DAVE 'THE BEAST'

BLOOD IS ONLY RED SWEAT

With Nick Towle

CONTENTS

Front-cover picture by Rob White of R.L White
Photography (www.rlwhitephotography.co.uk).

Cover Design by Jason Ferdinando.
www.elmhousepublishing.com

Published by
Elm House Publishing

Back-cover picture R.L White Photography.

Acknowledgements

I dedicate this book to my dad for always being there when I had problems in life. I am proud to have a father like him. Also, to my tablets and shining lights Angie, Carla and Becky for putting up with me through all the worry and the tears; and to my trainer and best friend George Probert for his loyalty and always being there for me through thick and thin: a true friend who has always believed in me.

Thanks also to my pals Ryan Vincent and Jim Daily for the 'prison-yard' work-outs I needed; and to Dave Platts, 'Leicester's notorious poacher'.

To Joe Wooly and Albert 'The Rat Man' Fox for the knuckle fights and the rat hunts (there ain't no rat safe with you guys around!).

Thank you Alan Hickingbottom for opening the boxing gym in Hemsworth and thanks for the free time you put in over the years. I wouldn't have been the man I am today if you hadn't opened that gym.

Thanks also to my cousin Alan Radford for the diets and the help with my fitness; to Trevor Callaghan, the best manager I ever had (if only I had had you from the start); to my trainer James Walker for the time he put in with me in the UK and abroad, and for kicking my arse when it needed kicking.A very, very big thanks to Craig 'The Clobberer' Smith, 'Nasty' Neil Coleman, Mark 'The Bull' Oates, John 'Pit Bull' Penn, Andy Cooper and Gav Keen for the broken knuckles, broken eye sockets, broken cheekbones, the fractured jaws, cracked ribs, the teeth knocked out, the broken noses, the cuts and the busted ear drums. There's been some good sparring over the years lads and Father Time will beat us all, but what I have had with you lads down the years you cannot buy. Thanks a million.

Thanks also to the Holmfirth boys Greg North, Andy Moorhouse and Brock and the Butlin brothers for their support; to my pal Pete Wiggins for the pads and the sparring over the years, and to you Dave Wiggins for your support.

Finally, thanks to all my family and supporters, and to Nick Towle for taking an interest in my story.

Foreword

Hemsworth is where I was born and it's almost certainly where I will die.

It's a small town but I call it a village because everyone knows everyone. A rough old place in many ways but it has a heart and, to me, it's the salt of the earth.

I feel it's important to introduce my home town before telling you my story as it's the backdrop to all the life-changing events, happy memories and tragedies that have shaped me as a man, a father and a fighter.

In many ways, I'm a chip off the old Hemsworth block: full of warmth but always ready to fight my corner when required.

According to the most recent census, there are now only 13,311 of us in our tiny corner of West Yorkshire. And, frankly, many of my townsfolk have seen better days.

Ours was once a one-industry town during the coal-mining years, but then the pits went in the 1980s and so did the livelihoods of many proud men.

Our town was one of many in Yorkshire which suffered greatly after Maggie closed the pits and shackled the unions. That's why we've always voted Labour up here. They used to say that Labour votes were weighed rather than counted in Hemsworth.

In the 80s and 90s, unemployment in our neck of the woods was sky-high and at one stage reached 50 per cent. Thousands of people on the bread line; the community ground into dust.

During those dark days there were entire estates where hardly anybody worked, and families had to scrimp and save just to survive. Many resorted to crime. Drugs and alcohol abuse became a problem.

Our patch was classed as one of the most deprived in Europe and loads of money came pouring in for regeneration schemes on the West End Estate and Scotch estate.

Since then, they've built the big Tesco store but there's

been way too much development and many of the good old watering holes have disappeared. Oh how green was my valley.

'The man is a fool who takes my kindness
as a sign of weakness'.

1) Roberto Duran and the Hands of Stone

I was getting a beating from the Hands of Stone and I could hardly breathe. The African heat was stifling; my lungs felt like they were about to burst. I was trying to take in gulps of air but the battery was relentless.

Big, heavy, murderous blows battered my kidneys; horrible, heavy scuds crashed into my temple. His jabs were cutting my face to bits; the quick one-twos were ripping my stomach. I'd feint to the right and he'd catch with me with a big left; I moved to the left and he slugged me with a right.

One right hook sent vibrations whizzing all the way down my spine, tingling the soles of my feet. For a second I was literally pinned to the spot. I was still reeling when he came in with more pile-drivers that knocked me back onto the ropes.

A sledgehammer was driven so hard into my chest it felt for a second like he was pulling his fist out of my rib cage. He was tearing a hole in my intestines with hellish blows thrown just at the right time. He seemed to know when my stomach was relaxed and then: WHAM! BAM! BAM! Three rockets fired into the bread basket that sucked the wind right out of me.

I was trying to parry the big shots as best I could, but it was no use: the man was too strong, too clever, too quick. Old Stone Hands was dishing out some proper medicine - the guy was playing me like a fiddle.

Another fizz-banger to the head almost warped my senses, nearly cleaned me right out. I was beginning to feel less than human. By the third round I was crying inside. My head was telling my legs: "Just go down."

Those thunder-slaps to my body were like flaming balls of hell. He'd drive one into my kidneys, then tear into my liver and heart. Every time he hit me with a vicious body punch I could feel the rake of his knuckles: it was as if he'd taken the gloves off. He was so powerful and his hand speed was from another planet. Quite frankly, I didn't know where I was or who I was.

I came out for the fourth and all hell broke loose. Duran was like a man possessed. He threw a demon hook into my chin that clamped my teeth together like a vice: I was in that halfway room between consciousness and Planet Zut. Then I heard chanting coming from a section of the crowd. I couldn't make out what they were singing at first.

"Manos de Piedra!" they hollered. What the hell did that mean?

I found out later that Manos de Piedra is what they call Duran in South America – it's Spanish for 'Hands of Stone'. To be honest, they're more like solid blocks of concrete.

Duran had mixed it with Hagler, Hearns and Leonard in his prime and given the boxing world some of its greatest fights. He'd risen from the slums of Panama to hold world-title belts at four different weights. He was older now and past his best, but, Suffering Jesus, could he unleash hell with those hands! He was a beast cut from granite with the heart of a lion

But when it came to heart, he'd met his match with me - and he knew it. For the next half-hour he threw shots at my head and body that nearly bent me over, but still I carried on. You have to kill me to beat me

In the final round I had nothing left. My legs had gone, the mind had fizzled out and still the blows came crashing into my skull, ripping into my soul. With 15 seconds to go he was strafing me. I grabbed hold of him and held on. Those last few moments felt like two hours: it's that dark other-world that only fighters know. It's at this point when everything closes in. There's just you and the other guy in this strange other-world.

There are times in a fight as brutal as this when you're completely alone, in a state of semi-consciousness. You're a child again. The monster's there but you can't see him, so you just thrash around and hope for the best. It's pure instinct. A sort of half-light gathers around you; the muffled sounds around the ring seem to belong to another world. There's just you and his face. His eyes bore a hole through your head: it seems he's been there your whole life.

Finally the bell went. There was no doubt who had won, but that didn't bother me: I'd gone the distance with a four-time world champion, one of the best there had ever been. Not only that, but despite the thorough beating I'd taken for most of the fight, I did have my moments. In the first round I really rocked Duran and had him on the ropes again in the fourth and seventh. Marvin Hagler, who was commentating for TV, was getting all excited.

"He's rocked Duran!" he screamed into the microphone. "Duran is hurt!"

'Marvellous Marvin' almost swallowed his mic and said Duran would have to keep his hands up or he'd be in trouble. The truth was, I *did* hurt him, but this only spurred him on more and he tore back into me even harder.

Duran is a down-to-earth fella and he admitted afterwards that I'd hurt him. In fact, a few years after the fight, he gave me a replica of one of his world-title belts as a mark of respect. On it, he had written: 'To Dave, you hurt me in Africa.' That meant a lot to me.

As soon as the fight was over, they had to carry me out of the ring because I was too exhausted to walk to the changing rooms. I was so beaten up I had to have a hernia operation afterwards.

Fighting a guy like Duran for eight rounds in that kind of heat takes more than just heart. In my case, it was a pig-headed refusal to buckle when everyone must have thought it was only a matter of time before I went down. I had absolutely nothing left in those final few rounds. I was beyond exhaustion.

When a guy like Duran is throwing bombs at you that could kill an ordinary man, and you're already spent, there's only one option left if your heart's big enough: hang on and pray to whichever god you believe in. I don't believe in any god - and I'm a stubborn old sod - so I keep dredging from the well though the well is almost dry.

I'd never been hit so hard in my life as I had been by

Duran that night in South Africa. It was by far the toughest fight I'd ever had. Maybe it's because you train so hard and for so long before a big fight that you carry on throwing and dodging punches when you're completely drained and only half-conscious. Apparently, in one fight I slugged a guy so hard it nearly knocked him off his feet. I say apparently, because I only knew what had happened when my mates told me afterwards. I had no recollection of it whatsoever: I was in the half-light again.

Early on in my career, I fought a professional who gave me such a beating he sent me into fairyland. The omens weren't good from the start: I climbed into the ring and fell on my arse as I came through the ropes. Right from the bell we were throwing proper big shots at each other. He was bigger and stronger than me and soon got on top. He rocked me with a vicious combination and I was in 'La La' Land. I was eight years' old again and standing beside the pie-and-pea van that used to stop by our estate when we were nippers. I was very small as a child and I was trying to jump up to see the pie-and-pea man. I said to my dad: "I didn't get my pie and peas!"

That's how far gone I was. The guy had knocked me back in time - and there were no bleeding pie and peas at the end of it.

2) The Beast in Me

I'm a simple man, a gentle man. I love my friends and family more than anything in the world. I have a lovely partner and two wonderful daughters.

I never swear in front of women – I get that from my dad. People see me as a bit of a softy, which in a way is true. But I'm also capable of giving someone a horrific beating if that is what's required.

I've never started a fight, but I've ended plenty. I have no anger and bear no grudges. I like to settle a dispute with a quiet word rather than a heavy fist. But the man is a fool who takes my kindness as a sign of weakness.

At my boxing club it breaks my heart to see the young ones when they're going at it. Sometimes I have to turn away - can't look. I don't even watch fights on TV anymore

I was a mummy's boy as a kid; hardly ever fought at school and wouldn't say boo to a goose. I never knew I could fight at all, to be honest, but then it began to dawn on me that I had to protect my brother and sisters – particularly my brother. He was gay. There were lots of blokes in Hemsworth who were gay but never let on. My brother came out of the closet early; my dad disapproved. He's a quiet bloke, my old man; a lovely fella - but this he could not understand.

Some nights there'd be trouble when blokes saw me out with my brother. Back in those days being gay didn't go down too well in our neck of the woods. One night, my eldest sister said there had been some trouble in the village and there was going to be a fight. I was just 16 and the guy who'd been picking on my brother was 45. No matter, I did him good and proper. It took one punch and down he went – TIMBERED.

Up until then I'd only had two fights, but when someone's taking the mickey out of your brother, you step in. From then on, I knew I could do damage. People can take the piss up to a point and then it's show time: The Gentleman becomes The Beast.

One day, my brother became my sister. Terry was now a woman called Kaye. She married a bloke; we got a lot of stick in the village. She can handle herself, our Kaye, but there's only so much you can take off people. I've never wanted to fight anyone for kicks, but if anyone messed with my family, particularly my kids, I'd tear their eyes out and smash their teeth in. It's just a dad thing.

I'm a great believer in the saying, 'An eye for an eye, a tooth for a tooth'. Once, when I was 17, two 15-year-old lads gave me a pasting, knocked the hell out of me. The next day I saw one of them; gave him a proper kicking. Dad was proud of me: all I ever wanted to do was make dad proud. We love each other a lot, me and dad, but he never shows his feelings. He's an old-school Yorkshireman. He kissed me for the first time recently, at my daughter's 21st birthday party.

Mam died of heart failure when I was 21. A sweeter woman you couldn't wish to meet - I loved her dearly. I lost my beloved nephew too: Gareth was more like a son to me.

Everyone's got their own crap to deal with, but in the fight game everything's so perfectly simple. It's just man against man, a straight test of strength and skill, and who has the biggest heart. There's no anger when I'm fighting, I'm totally relaxed. It's my heaven. This is what I enjoy and I believe I was born to do it.

On the 'outside', things aren't so simple - there are too many people wanting to have a pop at the Big Man. If someone gets clever in a bar, I maybe have a quiet word, but I prefer to walk away and let the dust settle: it takes a lot to make me angry. If they carry on gobbing and it makes them feel hard, so be it. Being a gentleman means a lot to me. If the worst comes to the worst and they won't take 'no' for an answer, then we go outside, but first I make them put £50 behind the bar. The reason? It's simple - if I get my shirt ripped, I want them to pay for a new one. I've lost count of the amount of times I've seen guys brawling in the street and they get their shirts ripped: it makes no sense to me. It kills me to see the old people out in town and they see all this bother from these idiots who fight with their shirts on. Some of them swell up when they see me out at night: they see a challenge. No problem - let's go outside and see who the better man is.

Once, down in Oxford, these two guys were giving me some bother in a bar. I was sat there with my mate George; we were minding our own business. These guys started getting shirty for some reason. I get this sometimes; maybe it's the way I look. They kept staring at me from the other side of the bar, so I looked away, but still they kept on looking, trying to put the spooks on us.

I pretended to look a bit scared, taking the piss. They came over to my side of the bar and I pretended to shiver. One of them came up to me and said: "What's the crack?"

"What do you mean?" I said.

But they meant business, these two. The only thing to do was to walk outside, but they followed us. I noticed that one of them, a really big lad, had a pint of Guinness in his hand. His mate was walking beside George and said to him: "Get your pal away from my mate 'cos he's gonna kill him.

George was walking behind me, with this guy in his ear. The big lad next to me gave me a funny look and smirked. He said: "Look at the size of you and look at the size of me."

What people like him don't realise is that it's not the size of the dog in the fight that counts, it's the fight in the dog. I actually told him that.

"Eh?" was all he said.

Clearly he still didn't get the message, so I thought I ought to show him what I meant. They were both stood together, him and his mate. I hit one with a left hook – that's the one I call Joseph. The other guy got clobbered with Herbert, the right. They were both timbered, fell straight to the ground like two sacks of shit. The man I'd clobbered with Herbert was trying to get back to his feet. I thought he was coming back at me, but he was saying he'd had enough

– just one punch and it was game over for him. The man who'd been pole-axed by Joseph was clean out. It looked to me like a paramedics job, so I put him in the recovery position and left. I hadn't wanted to harm them but this is how it goes sometimes.

There are other times when people need a damn good hiding because it's simple justice. I remember once, this guy who was known around town had nicked a purse from a lady in a supermarket. He was a slippery type, proper little rapscallion. There were people talking about taking a hammer to him; I was thinking more along the lines of giving him a good beating with the fists. I'd also heard, much to my annoyance, that he'd nicked £70 from his auntie's purse. His uncle, who knew me, called one Christmas morning and asked if I was still looking for him. I said yes.

He said the lad was in his house and did I want to come round? I finished my breakfast and told the missus I was just nipping out, wouldn't be long. I went round to the house and banged on the door.

The bloke and his missus were sat there in the kitchen; they pointed over to a settee where the little slime ball was sat. His jaw dropped a mile when he saw me. I went straight in with Joseph and Herbert. First I rattled him with Joseph and he screamed. Then I started driving my fists into his calves and ankles, and he cried like a child. I was working my way up his body: a Joseph smacked right into his rib cage; a Herbert ripped into his kidney. Then came a solar-plexus punch that drew the wind right out of him. I was giving him a severe beating but then his auntie appeared in the room and she started screaming too! It was a right bloody palaver, so I wished them a merry Christmas and did one. I'd been beating the little tyke for three minutes non-stop.

When I got back home my knuckles were red raw. But it was worth it and everybody got their money back. Sometimes there's nothing like a good beating to teach people the error of their ways.

18

There are some people who've done me wrong and might get away with it. There are others who've wronged people I know and respect, and they pay the price. It's instant justice: some people just have to be disciplined. When Joseph pays them a visit they tend not to forget it.

The only guy I know who can throw Joseph like me is 'Nasty Neil' Coleman – fantastic left hook. He's a cage fighter from Hemsworth and he's an absolute beast of a boxer too. I love to spar with the likes of Neil and Mark 'The Bull' Oates because I like to feel the punishment, the hurt, the bruising and the cuts on my face. It sounds silly but it's true – I call it 'medicine'.

I've had some right old scraps with the likes of Nasty, The Bull and Craig 'The Clobberer' Smith, but nobody has ever put me down in sparring. Something keeps me up no matter how bad the beating. I've sparred with guys weighing over 20 stone and none of them has ever knocked me down; I've been in the ring with people trying to kill me and still they can't put me away. I've taken many hard blows to the head. My memory is bad - *really* bad - but I can't give it up. It's my only addiction. Sometimes I've gone into fights knowing I'll get the crap beaten out of me. No matter – I just take the shots.

Street fighting's different: I usually just lay on a few punches and they're out. There's no fun in that. I can't stand the thought of the kids at my gym fighting in the street. I like to teach the young ones how to look after themselves but I very rarely watch them fight because it upsets me too much. I don't even watch fights on TV anymore: the prize ring is not what it was. I remember Hagler, Hearns and Duran in their prime. Steve Collins was another great and a true gent. I've met them all – fantastic fellas. Barry McGuigan's another one: a fantastic fighter and a smashing bloke to boot. What you see is what you get with Barry; he really is like he appears on TV. I've met him loads of times and he's commentated on a few of my fights. The man is an absolute comedian and a very clever guy. Yeah, he's alright, is Barry.

People used to say I'd be the next great middleweight, maybe even the next Hagler. I have the same style: rolling shoulders, chin tucked in, always on the front foot. But then I had the accident and everything changed. I couldn't get a licence to fight for a start.

I've met Hagler a few times. He spoke about me at a sportsmen's dinner in Sheffield; said I nearly put Duran down. Maybe so, but nearly is not good enough in the fight game.

3) Fate

What many people don't realise is that I wasn't even supposed to fight Duran: I'd been called up at the last minute as a replacement.

The guy he was supposed to fight, a South African called PJ Goosen, had injured his ankle in training and had to pull out just before the fight. I was plastering a bedroom wall at my sister Michelle's house in Hemsworth at 11 o'clock in the morning when I got a call from my trainer James Walker, who said he had some important news and wanted to meet me straight away at my house. I packed up my plastering trowel, float and stilts, and drove back to my house to meet James. I could tell with the excitement in his voice that he had something big to tell me, but I never imagined in a million years just *how* big. I pulled into the driveway and he was already there, grinning like a Cheshire cat. We went inside and he sat me down.

"Do you fancy going to fight in Africa?" he said.
I said yes, no problem, and asked him when.
"Tonight – we're flying from Heathrow at eight."
I half-smiled and wondered what the old bugger was up to: was it a wind-up?
"Do you want to know who you are fighting?"
"Who?"
"Roberto Duran!"
I started laughing, thinking he was having me on, but it was clear from the tone in his voice that he was deadly seriously. At first it just wouldn't sink in. Me versus Duran, one of the greatest fighters of all time? In Africa?

I packed my bags there and then as James watched over me, then we raced over to his house and he packed his. Then we darted down the M1 to Heathrow to catch a plane for South Africa. Three days later, on November 15, 1997, I'm in the ring with the Hands of Stone in Hammanskraal, near Pretoria, getting a thorough beating and loving every minute of it up until the last three rounds - they were hell.

Apparently, it was Duran's 100th professional fight and I could tell from the ferocity of his punches that he meant to mark the occasion in style. When I went eyeball-to-eyeball with him at the scratch, I was thinking: "Stop the world, I want to get off!"

But then I gathered myself, trying to seize the moment. It was a once-in-a-lifetime opportunity and I didn't want to waste it. As we tapped gloves I thought: "Just dig deep and do the best you can. He's an old guy – I'll be okay." I should have known better, but I had the slight cockiness of a young man back then, even in the presence a of a great.

When I got up close to him during those eight torturous rounds, I'd sneak in the odd snide comment, the cheekiest being: "No mas!" This means "no more" in Spanish and has particular significance where Roberto's concerned. It harks back to his re-match with Sugar Ray in 1980, their second scuffle in the famous trilogy. Duran had taken Leonard's WBC welterweight title off him five months earlier and Sugar wanted it back. After six-and-a-half rounds of intense battling, Leonard started showboating and got right on top of his man, goading and taunting Duran. In the eighth, Duran suddenly turned his back on Leonard, walked back to his corner and said to the referee: "No mas, no mas." The phrase has gone down in boxing folklore and I thought I might be able to use it to rile Duran, along with: "Come on you old bugger!" I'm not sure he liked that.

When the bell went for the end of the fight I held my arms aloft and walked back to my corner feeling 12ft tall despite the immense pain I was in. I couldn't believe I'd gone eight rounds with the great man. It was a special feeling and it'll never leave me. I was 28 at the time and I'd taken a year off work to concentrate on my boxing, so I was in peak physical shape. I needed to be too, otherwise Duran would have killed me. After going the distance with him, I became a local hero overnight. I felt like I could beat anyone now and was eyeing Neville Brown's British middleweight title. I was also planning a raid on the Central Area Middleweight belt.

The papers, local and national, were all over me after the fight in Africa and Sky Sports came over to Hemsworth to interview me. They brought the cameras over to my sister's house where a reporter interviewed me as I was doing some plastering – they were recreating the day I found out about the Duran fight. Then they did a live broadcast from my house and made it into a bit of a comedy sketch. As part of the comedy routine, the Sky team had arranged for my phone to ring and the moustachioed reporter picked it up. He said that Thomas Hearns - who once clonked Duran with one of the hardest knock-out punches I'd ever seen - was on the line and wanted to speak to me. I held my hands aloft, turned to the cameras, and hollered: "No mas!"

The Sky lads were pissing themselves at that one.

Those were heady days for me and the future appeared to be anything I wanted it to be. But, if truth be told, I never felt comfortable being out of work for so long and returned to my day job as a pipe-jacker. It was a fateful decision because, not too long after returning to work, I had the accident that changed my life and ended my professional boxing career. I was number nine in the country when I fought Duran, and this was at a time when the middleweight division included the likes of Chris Eubank, Nigel Benn and Michael Watson. Oh, how the mighty have fallen!

Everything had slotted perfectly into place until then. I had come through the amateur ranks and beaten some good guys, serious contenders. I'd also come back from a few beatings and took my defeats on the chin. I was under bad management in the early years and my record wasn't great, but then, in my late teens, I got myself a proper manager and things started to go my way. I was a rising star on the amateur glove scene under the guidance of James and Trevor Callaghan, my trainer/manager. I fought in France, Ireland, Denmark and Africa, and put some big guys away.

I won 18 of my 23 fights as an amateur before turning pro. With the help of James and Trevor – a wise old head who'd been in the game for donkey's years - I started doing some serious damage. Seven of my early professional fights ended in knock-outs and one fight in particular taught me that was I was ready to take on the big boys. It was a match-up with a guy called Rob Stevenson, when I was right at my peak. Early on in the fight I floored him with a big right. He got up on one knee but looked like he'd been hit by a juggernaut. I could tell he didn't want to carry on: he was stunned. The last time I saw a fighter with such a look of pure horror on their face was when I watched the George Foreman/Ken Norton fight as a nipper in '74. Norton had taken a severe beating from Foreman, who was in his prime and knocking people out for fun. There was one point in the fight when Norton, having just been on the end of one of Foreman's famous sledgehammer blows, looked like a terrified child in the presence of the Bogey Man. There was real terror in his eyes and you just knew he didn't want to carry on. It's strange how these big, strapping fellas seem to diminish in size when they're on the end of a good beating. When they're knocked to the canvas they appear so small and fragile, like pygmies in the shadow of giants. Stevenson had that same look about him when I pole-axed him with the Big Right. This was during my golden patch, when I won loads of fights on the bounce. In some I'd knock the guy down in under a minute. It was usually the Big Left that did the trick – good old Joseph.

I've always been renowned as a big puncher. When I strike them on the button with a crunching left hook they're usually straight down. I really do love my left hooks; there's really nothing like it when you land one on the sweet spot, right under the chin. I've never been a cricket fan but I guess it's a bit like how a batsman feels when he's just creamed one for four off the middle of the bat. It's the best feeling in the world.

When I've dropped my man with the Big Left I expect him to get up and fight, unless he's sparko. I have no time for people like Stevenson who go down at the drop of a hat. Why do these people not want to get up and fight? Surely it's every fighter's instinct.

4) Shovel Head

I had no fear going into the Duran fight. No-one scares me - except perhaps the missus.

The last time I was truly shitting myself going into a battle was when I had my first proper ring match at 17. You see, I wasn't meant to be fighting: I'd gone to a boxing night in Doncaster with my dad and was sat in the audience when a trainer came up to me and asked if I fancied getting in the ring.

He said he'd seen me fighting somewhere and liked what he'd seen. Apparently one of his boys' opponents hadn't shown up, so he asked me to step in. I accepted but didn't have a clue what I was doing. Somehow I ended up winning on points.

The next time I climbed through the ropes I met a real man, a tough nut from Doncaster called Mark Heardsely. He was known as Shovel Head.

The guy was huge. I saw him in the changing rooms before the fight: massive tree-trunk arms, huge biceps; all ripped muscle from top to toe. There were tattoos covering his entire body; I remember there was one of Bruce Lee on his knee cap.

I didn't have a clue who I'd be fighting because on those nights you could be up against any one of a dozen guys.

I thought to myself: "Who's the poor bugger fighting this guy?!"

Half an hour later, it all became clear - it was me!

There was no mistaking: it was right there in flashing lights - 'David Radford from Hemsworth Vs Mark Heardsley of Doncaster'.

This was my worst nightmare: Shovel Head was 11 years older than me and on his home turf. I ran upstairs to my dad in the crowd.

"I'm gonna get a hiding dad!" I roared.

The look on his face was pure horror. He was scared stiff, which made me even worse. But there was no way I was backing out. I jumped in the ring and within a minute I'd put Shovel Head on his arse. In the second round he came back at me, but in the third I got on top again and sent him back down to the canvas. He got back up and ended up going the distance with me. I lost on a very dodgy points decision - nobody could believe it. His manager offered me a re-match.

I may have lost that fight but it taught me a very valuable lesson: it doesn't matter how big and strong your opponent is - if you've got the heart, you can beat anyone. And I did beat him, everyone knew that. In the fight game you just have to accept that occasionally you're going to be at the mercy of judges who frankly don't know their arse from their elbow.

Clueless judges or not, it's just as important not to underestimate the little guys. I once fought a scrawny little kid at a country club and was so confident of beating him that I had a little wager with the owner of my local fish shop. I popped in one day before the fight and he said he'd give me the biggest fish in the shop if I won.

I said to him: "You might as well put that fish on now Arthur." I was so sure of beating the scrawny guy and when the day arrived I was really pumped up. I was ready to do serious damage to the midget and when the bell went I steamed straight into him. I threw three or four Josephs but missed with every one. I tried luring the little blighter in so I could release Herbert and floor him with a big right, but he was too quick and clever to fall for that. I missed with everything I threw, but he caught *me* more than enough times. The guy boxed my head off. I ended up losing on points.

So I didn't get my fish after all. I felt a bit of a dummy.

5) Beast versus Goat

As a natural-born beast, I have an affinity with animals which borders on the telepathic, but there have been times when we've crossed on the wrong path. On one such occasion, I chinned a goat.

I was living on an allotment in Hemsworth at the time, in a cramped old trailer I had 'found' in Folkestone (I think it had been nicked by a gipsy). You may well ask what the hell I was doing living in a trailer on an allotment site on the edge of town. The truth is, I'd just had an almighty row with the wife (we later divorced) and I needed to get away on my own for a while until things had calmed down.

I was as happy as a pig in muck in that trailer – until the Goat from Hell began spoiling my party. The little bugger, who lived on a plot of land next to where I'd parked the trailer, was keeping me awake at night with his constant braying and butting of this fence outside my pad. I put up with it for so long, but in the end there was only one thing for it: the goat would have to be disciplined.

One Sunday afternoon the damned swine was driving me bonkers. He just wouldn't stop butting the fence, which was only a yard away from the trailer. That was it: the red mist had descended and The Beast was back in town. I stormed out of the trailer in just my underpants and bounded over to where the goat was sticking his nut in the fence. Surprisingly, he didn't seem overly-concerned about the raging beast heading his way and gave me a look as if to say: "Yeah? And what the fuck do you want pal?"

BAM!

I clobbered Billy Goat with an almighty Joseph, a left-hook screamer that left him in a crumpled mess on the turf. He went down with a thud and was struggling to get back up. When he finally managed to get back on his hooves, his legs turned to putty and he fell straight back down. He was so weak on his legs he looked like one of those new-born lambs taking their first wobbly steps after leaving the womb.

I regretted what I had done instantly, so I stood by his side for what seemed like ages until he came round. When I was satisfied I hadn't done Billy Goat any permanent damage, I patted him on the head and went back inside the trailer to get some kip, but I felt so bad about what I'd done I couldn't drop off. And when I did finally manage to nod off I dreamt about goat's-head soup! So out of order that, hitting a goat.

Me and my four-legged pal were part of a little menagerie on the allotment site: there was The Beast in his trailer, a slightly dazed-looking Billy Goat and some chickens kept in a coop next to my plot. I was living by candlelight and occasionally I'd pop outside in the freezing night cold to light a fire and make tea, which I'd drink out of a glass milk bottle, the ones you used to get in the old days.

There were old boxes and all sorts inside the trailer, so I decided to empty the whole lot out - even the bed. Then I moved the chickens inside the trailer and took their place inside the coop. I wanted to test my mettle in the bitter cold: it was late summer but absolutely freezing at night.

To make sure the chickens were comfortable, I laid some straw down for them and then I had to work out my own sleeping arrangements in the coop. I made a bed out of straw bales and slung an old rug over me. Believe it or not, it was quite comfy, and now that Billy had been disciplined - needless to say, he didn't bother me again after being 'Josephed' - I actually slept much better than I did in the trailer. In fact, I was so comfortable I slept in the coop for three or four weeks, but then the stench of the place became unbearable and I had to go back to the missus and kiss and make up.

My body was in such good condition back then that I never felt the cold, even when it was sub-zero. My body was a finely-oiled machine, a solid insulator from the cold. I could sleep anywhere and work endless hours in any kind of weather.

Around about this time me and some workmates pitched up on a farm in Ilkeston, Derbyshire, where we were doing some pipe-fitting. It was deep mid-winter and we were staying in workers' 'sleepers' on the farm, which was run by a sweet old couple who treated me like one of their own. On one particularly freezing night, I decided to make things more interesting by sleeping in an old old lean-to – basically a barn without walls. I spread some straw out and got my head down under the milky moonlight. It was bloody freezing but I was in my mid-twenties and as tough as old boots.

I slept in the lean-to for several nights until the old farm lady saw me asleep on the straw one day and nearly had a coronary.

"Diesel!" cried the old girl. (She and her husband called me 'Diesel' because they reckoned I worked like an engine). "What are you doing on the straw?"

The poor lass was so aghast she ran back to her old fella to tell him there was someone asleep in the lean-to!

In the mornings, I'd get up with the cocks crowing, in the pitch black. There was a tap near my sleeping quarters which was used for watering the horses, but I decided to put it to another use – my daily bathing ritual, which became a strategic operation. First, so I could see what I was doing, I'd train the headlights of my blue Ford Orion on the tap area. Then I would grab some soap, take off all my clothes and wash myself down, sometimes under driving rain, gale-force winds and hailstone. Yeah, I was a proper hard bastard back then.

6) Goodnight Vienna

My face bears the scars of the business that I chose. I've taken some real beatings over the past 20 years and dished some out too. The ring and the cage are like life itself: who can take the pain and carry on?

There are plenty of people out there who see boxing as barbaric. They think fighters are brainless sluggers, but nothing could be further from the truth. It's one of the most highly-skilled sports around and there's no-one can sense human frailty like a good prize fighter.

So your man's got a dodgy eye? Hit him square in the socket.

Was he wincing slightly after throwing the big left? That must be a fractured finger. Let's make that five!

Broken nose? Smash his nasal bones to bits!

This may seem brutally simple, but it's far from easy to breach the defences of a skilled fighter without leaving yourself open to counter-attack. It's a game of chess: sometimes you guess what move he's gonna pull simply through years of experience. Other times, he'll completely bamboozle you with a move you didn't see coming in a million years. When it's your turn to attack, you've got to make sure your own defences are shut solid or it's Goodnight Vienna.

All a very skilled game, you see. No good taking an axe to your man's door; you've got to pick the lock instead – steal his game. Once you step inside that ring you need the cunning of a fox and the wiles of a coyote: brawn alone is not enough.

So please don't tell me boxing is barbaric. The true fight fans know this. They love nothing better than watching brain versus brawn – think Ali versus Foreman in Zaire. It was the shining example, a David-and-Goliath lesson in how to bring the big bad monster to its knees with nous and cunning.

At the end of the day, what fight fans really want is the

sweet smell of death in their nostrils. They implore you to fight to The End and that's why people like to watch me, because they know the other guy has got to kill me to beat me. Just like the matador, I try to give them what they want – the blood of the beast.

It's a natural human fascination, going right back to the ancient worlds, to watch two men going into battle with just fists for weapons. And how could it not be when you've got two guys, of roughly-equal strength, prepared to fight to the death?

But getting beaten up and taking it is just part of the act: it's the way you respond that decides whether you win or lose, or maybe even live or die. If your heart's big enough, you survive, no matter how bad the beating. If you're like me, you might even come back at the bastard with something twice as hard.

It's a bit of a cliché to say a fighter is at his most dangerous when he's hurt, but it's true. You're a wounded animal, and if that beast has any fight left, it can turn at any second, spring back to life though it seems almost dead. So long as the heart's still ticking and there's a sting in the tail, the danger remains until the last breath. Every good fighter has the ability to summon up the power for one last throw of the dice, maybe a scything blow or a counter-attack launched when you're on your last legs. I don't know where it comes from, but you dredge it up from somewhere. It's the magic source and not many have it.

I've lost count of the number of times I've snatched victory from the brink of complete exhaustion. Boxing is like no other sport in that you can go from humiliation to triumph in the time it takes to throw a good left hook. And it has to be said, I've been on the brink of humiliation more times than I care to remember, only to fight my way out of purgatory through sheer bloody-mindedness.

It was the special source that saved me from a good hiding from Geordie hard man Dave Johnson in '96. It was on his home turf in the North East, where the men are hard and the women are even harder. Now there's only one thing worse than getting a beating, and that's getting a beating on your man's turf. If his supporters are purring and he's in the mood, you've got problems. Some fighters are beaten before they even step inside the ring. The sight of hundreds of people crammed into a confined space, wishing you physical harm, can be overwhelming for some. But, at the end of the day, fuck 'em. Let's get this on and see who the better man is, then we'll see who's mouthing at the end of it. Once you start battling you've no sense of the crowd anyway; all you can hear is the odd shout from your corner men.

Now Geordies and Mackems have got some gob and they're very passionate in backing their man. Pack 'em inside an arena and they make a right bleeding racket. They were there in their thousands when I fought Johnson in Sunderland and they were expecting me to get a thumping. Johnson was a very good middleweight, one of the best in the country – some reckoned *the* best. I knew all about his record: 28 fights, 21 wins and three draws. He was only 24, two years younger than me, but he'd already boxed 180 rounds and put some good guys away. He'd lived in Newcastle and Durham but was a Sunderland supporter. When we got to Wearside they had these posters up declaring him 'The Real British Champion'. They said he was going to knock the shit out of me - I couldn't wait for the fight to start.

Going into the bout I was a bit knackered. I'd been in some brutal fights and they'd taken a heavy toll. Johnson, on the other hand, was in his prime. He was the confident one going into the fight and his guys knew it. The atmosphere in the run-up was incredibly tense. I thought a bit of light banter might lighten the mood, or maybe wind 'em up a bit more, so I wore a Newcastle United shirt, which drove the Mackems crazy. It's always nice to have a bit of fun now and again.

Johnson battered me in the third and fourth rounds. He was even better than I'd expected: quick jabs, big right, good left. He was fast and smooth with a good chin. I came out for the fifth and he rocked me with a big flurry. I went down on one knee but got back up. I barely had chance to draw breath when a big right came crashing into my rib cage, lifting me off the canvas. I was down on one knee again.

By this stage I was convinced I was gonna lose. He knew it too: I could see in his eyes that he thought I was done. And the beating only got worse: he was sending in some huge bombs and I was seriously hurt. He put me down again with a good body shot: I was spread-eagled on the ropes. We'd taken about 30 guys with us for the fight and they were all shouting: "Get up!"

"Piss off," I thought. "I'm not getting up 'til they start sweeping up!"

But get up I did. As I've said before, a good fighter is very dangerous when he's hurt. When he's injured and surrounded by his friends, he's a hooded cobra being poked with a stick. I knew my mates were expecting me to do the business, so I had to find a way of mastering this man who was giving me such a hiding. I knew I couldn't last another round with him - never mind another six - so I had to find something from somewhere to end it quickly.

Now when you've been floored by a haymaker and you get back up, the next few seconds are vital. The other guy's primed like a matador with the bloodied beast at his mercy. You, on the other hand, have entered the dark corridor: the well is dry and the legs have gone – you're in survival mode. You get back on your feet and you start wobbling: you're in the danger zone. You have to get your arse out of there pronto. First, you make sure that if you're going to land anything, it's hard and fast, otherwise you're going straight back down – no question.

As I got back up I was still clinging to the ropes. He came in to finish me off. First I sent a strong right into his body; he held onto me. Then came the left hook to his chin and down he went. Game over in the fifth round.

Johnson spent three days in hospital after that and never fought again. It's a funny old game: he'd battered me in that fight and should have walked it, but, from the moment the bell went, I had this strange sense that someone, or something, was watching over me. I don't believe in any god but if there is something up there guiding us, it certainly had a hand in that fight. It was an odd feeling and I'd never had it before – nor have I since - but throughout those five rounds of severe punishment I definitely felt as if someone had a hand on my shoulder. Even the hardest bastards need a helping hand sometimes!

Divine intervention aside, there's nothing anyone can do once you're inside those ropes – not your corner men, your fans nor your friends. You know at the back of your mind that your mates are out there in the crowd and it gives you a tremendous lift, but they can shout all they want – they're just spectators at the end of the day. To put it bluntly, you're on your own pal. Occasionally, your corner men can bring you out of a slump with a bark in the ear or a quiet pearl of wisdom. After one particularly-brutal round with Johnson, I slumped back to my corner all washed up. My head was cut and I was so knackered I didn't know whether it was Saturday, Sunday or Easter Monday. For a gee-up, my corner man James Walker gave me a slap round the face and told me I was throwing punches that wouldn't hurt his missus. It was his way of bringing The Beast out of its cage – and it worked.

7) Two Tribes

If the likes of Shovel Head used to scare me when I was young, they held no fear for me as I got a bit older.

In fact I would have relished fighting Shovel Head when I'd reached my proper fighting weight. I was knocking out some big names by my mid-20s and taking on, and beating, men who were supposed to be a class above me.

Everybody down our way wanted to see me fight local star Dave Larkin, who was from South Kirby, a town near Hemsworth. There was a lot of rivalry between the two towns back then - there still is, in fact - and if the fight could be arranged it would not just be a contest between me and Larkin, but a settling of old scores between the two 'villages', as I like to call them. The towns up our way are pretty tribal and much of it stems from the miners' strike in '84. In those days there was a lot of bad blood not just between the villages, but whole communities. Even families were split down the middle. There were those who carried on working through the stoppages (they were known as 'scabs'), and those who laid down their tools and refused to go back to work until Maggie had been ousted – fat chance of that.

People never forget around here and the divisions that existed then are still there today. Communities like ours never really recovered from those dark days and the hatreds have festered ever since. Our 'village' has never got on with Kirby, a town just a bit smaller than ours but with a similar history. The pit there was sunk in 1881 and closed in 1988, with the loss of 3,000 jobs. Other pits went too: Frickley, Grimethorpe, Kinsley Drift Mine (built on the site of the old Hemsworth Colliery, which closed in 1977). Thousands of proud working men left on the scrapheap; entire families skirting the breadline. It's hard to describe the effect this had on the people around here. Maggie and the Tories robbed them of what we should all have a right to – hope.

So anyone who knows anything about the history of

Hemsworth and South Kirby will know why my fight with Larkin, in April 1996, was more like a war between two towns, with me and Larkin the standard-bearers for each tribe. We hated them and they hated us. I was convinced there'd be a massacre on the day.

I was actually supposed to be fighting another guy but he pulled out and Larkin stepped in. I didn't like it one bit because I knew what could happen when you get a load of Hemsworth lads and South Kirby fellas under one roof. Larkin was a very highly-rated kid with 60 fights and a few ABA titles to his name: the bee's knees, then, on the amateur circuit. He was 10 years young than me and - on paper at least - a class above.

There was a lot of gobbing from both camps beforehand and each village was sounding off against the other. Lots of very angry and very vengeful people went to that fight – you felt it just had to kick off. Me and Larkin, a nice kid, were caught in the crossfire and our townsfolk never passed up an opportunity to tell us how important it was to win. At the weigh-in, the atmosphere was so tense you felt it might explode. At one point Larkin's trainer came up to me and offered me his hand, but I looked the other way because I was so angry that the fight was going ahead.

The Wakefield Metrodome was packed to the rafters on that night. It was an eight-rounder and went the distance. Though I didn't knock Larkin out, I won every round. On paper there was no way I should have won, but I was fighting with anger that day because, to my mind, the fight should never have happened. As it turned out, there wasn't a bit of trouble in the crowd and everyone was on their best behaviour.

Back then I was putting blokes away who should really have taken me to the cleaners. I trained so hard that I had the fitness to go the distance with guys who might otherwise have given me a pummelling. I'd get up at 5am every morning and do a four or an eight-mile run. Then I'd go to work and, after I'd finished my shift, go straight to the gym for pad-and-bag training. It was an 18-hour day in all. At night, I had all these endorphins whizzing round my body and it was hard to sleep. Yet I was never tired: I was living on all the energy I'd built up during the day. I was as fit as a racehorse back then.

Before a big fight I'd ratchet up the training a step further – and that's when my dear old cousin Alan Radford's wicked prison work-outs came to the fore. They really were something else and I'll forever be indebted to my cousin for giving up his time to put me through hell. For anyone not familiar with prison work-outs, you're basically taking your body to the brink during each one or two-hour session, and the punishment gets harder the further you get into the programme. You do a minute's press-ups then a bleeper goes and you're doing sit-ups while the trainer-from-hell is sat on top of you, barking instructions into your lug-hole. Another bleep and you've got the dreaded medicine ball in your hands. You've got to stoop down and weave the bloody thing back and forth between your legs; then do sit-ups with it: up and to the left, down again; up and to the right, down again. And so on and so forth until another beep. Then it's more press-ups, more sit-ups; another bloody round with the medicine ball. Then the kettle-bell comes out. Then the medicine ball again, with Alan stood on my toes shouting: "Quicker! QUICKER!! Feed me the bloody ball!"

It's knackering work, but if you've got the guts to get through it, it's worth every drop of sweat. I was really fighting fit when I was on the prison work-outs. Our Alan was a genius at getting me into shape. In the week before a fight I'd do three prison work-outs a week – bleeding agony. All the energy I was burning gave me a ferocious appetite, which would have been okay ordinarily, but not when you're trying to keep the pounds down to make the weight. Resisting the grub is hard enough at the best of times, but when Alan came along he paid special attention to my diet. No garbage was allowed in the run-up to a bout: it was all greens, pastas, oily fish and fresh fruit. Booze was basically a no-no too. With James Walker's training and our Alan priming me up, I was a lean fighting machine ready to take on the world – and then disaster struck.

8) Completely and utterly shafted

On August 18, 1998, my life changed forever. I usually get a sense when something out of the ordinary is about to happen, but on that day I had no premonition at all.

I was shaft-sinking for an Irish firm on a site in Huddersfield and had started the shift at 7am as usual. There were four of us down there cleaning the shaft - me, my mate John Delaney, a bloke we called 'Patsy Nightmare' and a lovely Irish kid named Joe. By about dinnertime we were more than 40ft down and the shaft was being sunk 4ft to 5ft at a time while we were below the collar.

With shaft-sinking you dig a bit away and then push, dig a bit more and then push again. But we were being rushed by Patsy Nightmare, a blue-eyed boy who earned his nickname because he was always in too much of a hurry and seemed to do whatever the hell he liked. He was digging out far too much at a time: it was all rush, rush, rush with Patsy Nightmare. Now anyone in that line of work will tell you that you should never push in those shafts when there's someone below the collar. I remember thinking that it might get a bit awkward when we next push because there were too many segments above us. Suddenly Nightmare shouted: "Dave, we're gonna push."

I carried on working because I knew the cage would take about five minutes to drop down to us at the bottom. Nightmare should have sent the cage down first and then pushed, but he didn't. John thought the cage was about to come down and got out of the machine. Then: WHOOSH! We heard this strange, sucking sound like something was dropping down. John, who had never been down a shaft before, looked over at me and we burst out laughing. Then, all of a sudden, two metal 'shoes' came down on us. When they hit us, travelling at 60 miles an hour, they literally weighed a ton. I was struck on the head and shoulder; John was hit by the other shoe and broke his back. There was so much blood spattered around the shaft that a 6in water table had turned completely red. I remember telling my mates that

I'd hurt my arm and asked them to help me up, but on no account should they touch my collarbone, which I knew was broken. That's the last thing I remember other than a vague recollection of being surrounded by paramedics and being stretchered out of the shaft.

One of the men working up top, a lad called Ian who I still work alongside today, later told me he'd dialled 999 as soon as he saw the shoes coming down. He looked down the shaft and saw me hobbling around, then I just hunched down with my arms crossed. Everyone stayed put apart from Patsy Nightmare, who fucked off in his van.

Everything about that incident I've had relayed to me after the event because I'd lost consciousness. Apparently I'd said to the paramedics that I was okay, just get me out. I must have been unconscious because I hardly remember anything of the paramedics coming down. All I remember are faces peering down at me, the blood-red water and John being tended to. I cracked a few jokes to the paramedics. Then the lights went out.

Ian came to see me in hospital a few days after the accident and said: "You were hit by a ton of metal and you still didn't fucking go down!"

Me and John were rushed to Huddersfield Royal Infirmary and taken straight to intensive care. I remember nothing of my first day in there but one of the nurses, whose husband Andy Moorhouse comes to watch my bare-knuckle fights, was on duty that day and she recalls everything like it was yesterday. She said my injuries were horrific: a broken collarbone, shattered jaw, six fractured vertebrae and two broken ribs. Oh, and I lost some teeth as well.

It looked touch and go for a while but I had age and fitness on my side and was out of intensive care within two days. I was kept in for another 11 days but I was out of the woods, which is more than can be said for my poor friend John. He'd snapped his back beyond repair and would be paralysed for life.

When I got out of the infirmary my mind and body were shot to bits. My back was absolutely knackered (still is). I had to take two years off work – it was the longest two years of my life. To get back to work I had to pass a medical. I had the examination but the doctors told me I couldn't start grafting again for another six months. It totally crushed me. How could I be a man without work? A terrible depression set in during those endless weeks and months sat doing nothing at home. I had always been a worker; my dad was a worker and my grandfathers were grafters too. It was in the blood: even when I turned professional I carried on grafting. I just couldn't live without it. And here I was, home alone, with the wife at work and the kids at school. Everything just stopped dead; even walking around the house was a struggle. My back was so fucked I had to use a walking stick, but whenever I managed to make it out of the house I refused to use one out of sheer stubbornness.

The physical side of my suffering was bad enough, but then my head started to go too - oh dear. The worst part for me was thinking that people might suspect I was swinging the lead just to collect my sick pay, so I went back to hospital for another medical. The doctor asked me if I could bend down and touch my toes. So what did I do? I jumped up and started doing press-ups!

"I'm as fit as a fiddle mate," I lied.

A couple of weeks later I went for my final check-up and they still wouldn't give me the go-ahead for work. It meant I'd have to sit it out for the full six months. There was no way I'd be able to do that and retain my sanity, so I rang Ian, who was working for another firm at the time, and asked if there was any work going. He said, "give me half an hour" and, within an hour, he rang back and said I could start with his firm straight away. I struggled at first but soon got the hang of it again and, within three months, I was in charge of a gang doing some work on railway embankments. I did a spell in London then found work in Wakefield with another Irish firm run by a nasty old Paddy who was always falling out with his two sons. I was working alongside my old mate Screaming Skull, block-beaming bungalows. The Irishman's sons were only doing one or two a week, but me and George knew the score straight away and were doing five a week in no time. That pissed Paddy off no end.

Though I was back in the saddle at work, my professional boxing career was over. My injuries were so bad I was stripped of my licence. My trainer Trevor Callaghan, who was one of the main men on the British Boxing Board of Control, told me I wouldn't be able to fight again professionally. It was a real bummer but I had to take it on the chin. I don't blame Trevor one bit. It was the right decision and he was only thinking of my health, but I was so bitter at the loss of my career when I was really going places and, up until the accident, in peak physical condition. The only reason I'd survived the accident was because I was so fit and strong. In fact, the metal shoe probably came off worse than me!

Seriously, that collision would have killed any normal man, but the tragedy is that it should not have happened in the first place. There should have been pins inserted in the plant which would have stopped those damned shoes from coming down on us. It's standard procedure, but, of the four shoes in operation that day, two of them fell in. The other two had ropes attached to them which had stopped them falling. Just as well really, because if they hadn't, there'd have been four men going to hospital instead of two.

Poor old John: he'll be confined to a wheelchair for the rest of his life. I was the lucky one. I should have died that day, but it just wasn't to be. I reckon someone must have been looking down on me again - it could only have been Mam. The funny thing is, she was born not far from that site in Huddersfield. What else could have saved me from a big lump of metal travelling at 60 miles an hour?

A few days after the accident, a doctor came to have a look at my shattered arm as I was lying in my hospital bed. I could see from his face that despite all the horrific stuff he must have seen down the years, he was appalled by the extent of my injuries. I noticed he did a double take when he saw the huge tear in my skin where the metal had ripped my collarbone apart. The hole was so wide the doctor could get his entire hand inside the hollow flesh. It was a pitiful site.

Truth is, I've never really recovered from that accident. And probably never will.

9) Nasty Neil

When you've sleep-walked your way through two whole years of your life, it's not easy getting back into the fold.

It's like spending 24 months cooped up inside a darkened room, then one day you decide to open the shutters, draw back the curtains and step out into the sunlight, blinking.

Everything is somehow not what it was. More to the point, *you* are not quite what you were. It's a weird, almost hallucinogenic, feeling. On the one hand, you feel like you're getting your mind and body back to something like working order, but on the other, you feel cast adrift from everything that once made you feel safe in a hostile world. Ask anyone who's spent long enough in the trough and they'll all tell you the same thing: there are no certainties any more. White is black and black is white.

But there are certain things that put your own problems in perspective, and salvation comes when you least expect it. Sure enough, one day something happened that shook me straight out of the slump - I saved a baby's life.

It happened one Sunday morning, when I saw a car on fire at the bottom of our street. I rushed over to the flaming vehicle and saw a baby inside, strapped to a child seat. Another guy was on the scene too and together we managed to break into the car and get the child off the back seat. I pulled the seat-belt strap off the baby chair and we pulled the kid to safety. I ran back to my house and by the time I'd reached the front gate, I heard a massive explosion. I turned round and saw the car turn into a massive fireball, just minutes after we had got the baby out of the vehicle. I stayed in the street until the ambulance arrived and, when it drove off, I swore there and then that if the kid survived I'd get off my arse and get on with my life.

The baby ended up losing a leg from the knee down and the other foot, but survived. Within a few weeks of hearing the news, I was back in the ring again. I knew I couldn't get my boxing licence back because of all the terrible injuries

I'd suffered in the accident, but then the cage people and the unlicensed-boxing fixers came calling. I was offered an unlicensed fight and I accepted - no questions asked. Funnily enough, I had to go back underground to carry on doing the thing that I loved the most.

But it was the bare-knuckle scene that really got me going. It had fascinated me for ages; this sport that was stripped down to its bare bones. It was a blessing for me: I'd already been bare-fist sparring with the heavies at the gym, so naturally I took to it like a duck to water. I was home again!

Now, I'd never really had to take any knuckle punches in the street because I'd just lay on one or two Herberts and they'd be spark out. But then I started sparring with some proper nasty bastards in the gym and discovered that taking a good knuckle shot - one that shakes you right down to the bones - and carrying on through gritted teeth is the mark of a true man. I'd got the bug!

You really do need the heart of a lion to make it in the knuckle world. It's nothing like pub-fighting: it has rules, it has a 'ring'; it's an arena for the bravest men, not bar-room bullies. You have to be a born fighter to survive in this game.

To be honest, I've never classed myself as a fighter as such, but I must have been born with a fighter's heart. Some days I'd go sparring knowing me and the other guy would knock the absolute crap out of each other. In one particularly nasty session, I broke my nose so badly it became almost unrecognisable as my own. I've had seven or eight practice partners since then and it's still broken.

In some ways it's a terrible thing, what we do, but no matter how bad the punishment, I'm always hungry for the medicine. I'm lucky in that I have so many mates who are ready and willing to dish out spoonfuls of my favourite remedy. I know a lot of very hard men who can lay it on thick, but the ones I trade with only show their beastliness inside the ring or the cage. Most of them are little pussy cats on the 'outside' - you only have to ask their missus!

The only man who's wobbled me in the gym is 'Nasty Neil' Coleman. He's seriously hurt me out in the fields as well. When it comes to dishing out serious punishment, Mr Coleman more than cuts the mustard! It's the double hook that works wonders for him – a ferocious weapon.

Andy Cooper is another local lad you don't want to mess with. He's an absolute gent, but put him inside the ring or the cage and, boy, what a nasty bleeder. We used to fight each other in a cellar below the gym – no rules. We didn't quite kill each other, but it was fun trying.

Andy's a cage man through and through, an ex-British champion. He trades in elbows, knees, fists, choking, stamping and spiking. The Cage is a brute.

I was also sparring with a guy from Ackworth called Gav Keen who used to give my legs so much hammer that they'd be black by the end of it. The bruising was so severe it took weeks to heal. Gav's a hard lad and so is Andy, but Nasty Neil is something else. He's got one of the most ferocious left hooks I've ever come across and he's managed to break my cheekbone twice. He's also rearranged my snout on numerous occasions. When he hits you square in the eye, the pain is devastating. And if you show any sign of weakness - and he senses you're hurt - he'll tear you to pieces, seriously.

I must have had hundreds of sessions with The Nasty One and they've all been truly gruesome. In a normal session I'll lose about two pints of blood.

The longest we've ever gone in a single spar down in the cellar is 55 minutes. That one was proper hard-core stuff: head-butting, elbowing, kicking each other's shins to bits. The blows were struck so hard we could hear our shins squelch as we moved around the room. After nearly an hour of beating the shit out of each other, we were so knackered we had to lean on each other as we walked out of the gym – it was the only way we could stop ourselves falling over.

I've never fought anyone as long as long as I've fought Nasty in a single session. There are no rules, no breaks and there's certainly no mercy. It's constant battery, mates trading heavy blows. And, yes, we are good friends. It may seem crazy that two mates should want to do so much damage to each other, and I have to admit that if anybody walked in on us during those sessions they'd probably think it had gotten out of hand and try to stop it. Honestly, if you saw us down there in that basement, you'd probably think: "Bloody hell, they're trying to kill each other!"

Neither of us was prepared to give an inch, no matter how bad the beating.

But, as crazy as it seems, there *is* an element of control to our sessions and we know just how far to take it before it gets out of control. It's an exercise in discipline and stress relief for both of us. We call it 'medicine' because it's an instant cure for our ills. After a session we're both left with cuts and marks all over our bodies. I've usually got these big lumps on my shin where I've been blocking kicks – bone-on-bone collisions that make a nice cracking sound. There's nothing like the pain of blocking kicks with your shins, especially when The Nasty One is pummelling your eye with his fist. Unlike Neil, who was a trained cage fighter, my legs weren't conditioned for that sort of punishment. It meant I just had to take the pain and carry on. Sometimes I'd be fighting with a broken eye socket as well. I could tell when Neil had broken my socket because it would jut out of my head at a hideous angle.

When he had me pinned to the ground and there was nothing else I could do to get myself out of the situation, I'd introduce the Crow Peck (along with a few sharp elbows!). Crow-pecking is where you rap on the top of your man's head with the sharp ends of your hand's metacarpal bones.

When your man's got you down and you can't disentangle yourself, the Crow Peck is your only chance. It's the final resort, like the cage version of Custer's Last Stand. It's not only very irritating for the receiver, but it hurts like hell too. You know that if you peck your man hard enough, it might force a submission.

I resort to crow-pecking when the fists are not doing enough to force the submission. As we're pecking away at each other, me and Nasty will be laughing our heads off. One of us might decide to use the Fish Hook as well. This is when you're down on the floor and you *really* need to hurt your man. The Fish Hook takes the fight back to a primitive state: you wedge two fingers inside your man's mouth and pull like mad at his gums. What you're doing is stretching his mouth back until the pain becomes so intense you might win a submission. This is just one of a number of savage methods to bring a nasty man to heal.

Now some may ask why we enjoy taking such a beating. For me, I think it's a form of self-punishment: I punish myself for not saying the things I want to say to people in everyday life. I'm so easy-going that when people say things to me that I think are out of order, I don't retaliate. I keep my mouth shut when I know I should be saying something to let them know they've upset me. Or perhaps I'm just trying to get all that human meanness knocked out of me; cop a load of scuds off Nasty 'til I can't take no more. I've never been an aggressive man but I know there are dark forces at work down there somewhere.

And then there's mam and Gareth – always a factor. I would like to blame God for my loss but I can't because I don't believe in the guy. Surely, if there *was* a god, he wouldn't have dimmed the lights on those two stars. And yet I have to blame someone for my loss and that someone is probably me. It may seem crazy, but it's hard to rationalise these things when you've experienced such a massive bereavement twice over. I'm convinced I'm still in the grieving process and maybe those punishment sessions with Neil are my way of trying to overcome the grief. When I'm down there in the cellar with Nasty, taking all those heavy shots in fights that seem to last an eternity, I can feel all the frustration oozing out of my pores, along with a quarter-gallon of blood. It's the frustration of all those years bottling things up and keeping schtum when I should have been giving people a piece of my mind. In any case, I love fighting the likes of Neil, Andy, Gav and The Bull, because they know you like it that little bit harder - and they always oblige. It's easy to fire Neil up: I tell him my missus has hit me harder.

"Step it up a bit Neil!" I'll shout through my gum shield, when really I'm hurting like hell.

"Come on, soft lad, I haven't even got a busted nose yet!"

I'll tell him his punches aren't hard enough to break popcorn – that really stirs the shit storm. He'll start savaging me like a rabid dog. During one fight I called him a nasty bleeder and the name stuck.

He was sending rockets into my face that came in so hard and fast it felt like being hit by seven people at once. He fractured my left eye socket so badly it took about five weeks to heal, then I was back at it.

Fighters like Neil are a rare breed. Some people who call themselves fighters are not worthy of the name. I remember hitting one guy in the first round of a glove match and he went down like a roll of lino. He got up on one knee but I could tell he didn't want to carry on. No heart: clearly in the wrong game son.

I like to be in the ring with a fighter like me: big heart, packs a punch and can take one. Never gives up. Fights to the death. A warrior.

10) The Scorpion and the Toad

I've always been handy with the gloves off. I had my first ever fight against a school bully who'd hit a girl, a friend of mine.

He was a biggish lad, this bully, but I sorted him in seconds with a head-butt and a couple of meaty blows to the chin. Fettling someone like that wasn't something I'd ever dreamt of doing before, but I found myself acting on instinct. It also taught me that the head could be a valuable weapon.

I also discovered at a young age that using every weapon at your disposal would come in very handy in 'street' fights, and by this I mean anywhere outside the ring. I'm not proud to admit this, but I've had plenty of them. I can honestly say I've not started a single one and physical violence is an absolute last resort. But if push comes to shove and there's no other way to resolve the issue at hand, the fighting instinct kicks in and I wouldn't think twice about using the head, the elbows or the knees. Anything goes when the situation requires it.

When I look back, the street fights that maybe could have been avoided are the ones I regret the most. There are others that I don't regret one bit – they're the ones where I've had to discipline people who've gotten out of hand or disrespected my friends or family. I've had about 100 street fights in total and won every one. There have been times when I've hit someone in the pub after they've got out of line or swelled up just because they know I'm a fighter. Two or three days later, I'm depressed just thinking about it. You see, no matter what these people have said or done, I know they're not in my league as a fighter and I should have tried harder to defuse the situation when it kicked off.

But I only *respond* to threats; I never make them unless it's absolutely necessary. This is probably the reason I've only ever been in trouble once with the cops despite getting involved in so many street scuffles. I've never liked to cause trouble but sometimes it just comes my way.

The bother has slowed down in recent years and I reckon it has a lot to do with people watching my bare-knuckle fights on the internet. Most of them have been posted on Youtube and tens of thousands view them. I didn't like the idea of my fights going on the internet at first, but looking back, I think that people who might once have fancied their chances against me have a lot more respect for me now they've seen some of the ferocious bare-knuckle dust-ups I've had down the years. Certainly those who have watched those scraps would surely know they'd be in for a difficult time if they started anything. I imagine the people who knew me as a kid will see those images of me scrapping with my eyes popping out and scars on my head, and know that this once-good-looking young man had been in a scrape or two. They probably don't understand why I'm still doing it after all the hammer I've taken and the memory loss, but perhaps they've never had an addiction.

Not one of my street fights has gone on longer than the time it takes to throw two or three punches. This has been the case since my final year at school, like the time I caned that bully who thought he was the bee's knees. These people used to get the shock of their lives when they saw this scrawny, quiet little kid with the choir-boy looks suddenly explode and put them away. And, by jingo, I really used to do the business. They would always make the mistake of seeing that baby face as an invitation to give me a hiding, maybe show off in front of their girlfriends. All of a sudden I was knocking out fellas twice my size and twice my age – it was like shelling peas! Seriously, I couldn't believe how *easy* it was, and it was as much a surprise to me as anyone. It all started coming together for me when I was about 16 or 17. I would wait for the inevitable phone call from one of my sisters reporting some trouble down at the pub and off I'd go to sort it out. That's what happens when you've got four sisters – and now two daughters.

Back when I was still a fledgling and not properly filled out, there was many a time when some guy would hurl abuse at me as I walked down the street. They must have thought that my reputation was a myth. A little baby-faced boy knocking out grown men? Pull the other one!

They just wouldn't have it. Each and every one of them probably thought they'd be the man to bust the myth – but none ever did. They would try to scare and belittle me, but I've never feared any man in a fight. The threat of violence can be terrifying for some; to me it's just a situation to be dealt with. I never panic. A big man causing bother might set others shaking - I just concentrate on his jaw. Where there's a big man, there's a big jaw to be broken.

And I've broken many, many a jaw. When I'm walking through town nowadays I look around and see all these people whose jaws I've fractured. I was once sat in a café with a workmate, having some breakfast, and two stocky guys walked in preening like peacocks. They looked at me and their looks changed instantly. One of them had been on the end of a Beast left hook after shouting his mouth off one night. I turned round to my mate in the cafe and said: "See that guy, I broke his jaw once." He didn't even raise an eyebrow.

I was never any more than 11st up to being 24, but then I started putting weight on and The Big Beast started to emerge. I never like to crow but when I was at my top weight I was unbeatable on the street. Sometimes I'd put more than one man away in a single brawl, like the time I disciplined three loud-mouth drunks one Saturday afternoon in Barnsley. I was doing some pipe-jacking work and one of them pissed on me through a fence. I leapt to my feet and immediately put one of them down with a left hook, then pole-axed his mate with a right cross. The third guy grabbed me and tried to bite me. At the same time, one of the guys I'd just flattened was trying to get back up. I kicked him straight in the chops and the guy who was trying to bite me was floored by a head butt. Then I left-hooked the guy trying to get back up and kicked him in the face again. One more left hook to the jaw and he was spark out. All three of them were laid out like skittles in a bowling alley.

So yes, jaws are my speciality. I think it's because I love

throwing the left hook and the uppercut. There was one time when the jaw of a local footballer - a proper big mouth who thought he was King Kong – got in the way of a Beast Special. He was a lot quieter after that. It's not easy being gobby when you've just had your jaw broken in two places.

The thing with me is, I'm an old-fashioned type and like to see myself as the protector of the brood. In my eyes, anyone can be a danger to the nest. When I see a big, hulking fella walk through the doors of a pub or step into the ring with me, I don't necessarily see a dangerous man. For me, a dangerous man could just as easily be a midget or a scrawny guy with specks on. Anyone taller than 5ft and weighing over 10st has the potential to be a dangerous man in my book – I take no chances. I've known 20st men who couldn't land a decent punch if their life depended on it. They're built like tree trunks but snap like the most delicate of flowers. I've also known squeaky-voiced saplings who could tear you limb from limb. Personally, I love to test myself against all types: the brutes, the giants, the box-clever, savvy types; the sluggers, the artful dodgers, the dancers, the wily devils and, sometimes, the scum of the earth. Deep down, I know that what I'm doing is wrong (suffering Jesus, the missus has reminded me enough times!), but I simply can't get enough of it. It's like that old tale about the Scorpion and the Toad. The two creatures meet on the edge of a riverbank and both need to get to the other side, but only the toad can swim. The scorpion asks the toad if he can hop on his back to the other side and at first the toad refuses. But the scorpion assures the toad that he won't sting him because, if he did, they'd both drown. So the toad agrees to give the scorpion a lift across the river. They get halfway across and the scorpion appears to have been true to his word, but then the toad feels a sharp pain in his back. The scorpion has fatally wounded him. The toad loses strength and slips beneath the surface, dragging the scorpion down with him to their watery grave.

The scorpion had made it halfway across the river but killed the only thing that could have got him to safety, even though it meant dying a horrible death. It's nonsensical, but in many ways I think it sums up human nature: we act on impulse; we are governed by forces beyond our control. We are, by our very nature, self-destructive and drawn to the very things we know will probably kill us. I am the scorpion in this tale (in other words, my own worst enemy), but I'm also the toad. Both creatures have their own fatal weaknesses and both, against their better judgement, decide on a course of action which they know might be their last. Like the scorpion, I am naturally impulsive, sometimes for the worse. And like the toad, I cannot say no, particularly to the offer of a fight. It might be a cage bout, a ring fight or a bare-knuckle scuffle – makes no difference to me. I'd fight King Kong if you got me a pair of stilts.

Basically, if they ask, I fight. Several times I've agreed to a scrap at the drop of a hat and sometimes I've jumped in at the last minute.

On July 16, 2005, I took on world cage-fighting champion Michael Bisping after his opponent dropped out just days before the show. Bisping was mortified that his man had pulled out, so the MMA (mixed martial arts) guys asked me if I wanted to fight him. I said yes despite never having been in The Cage before. I was in my late 30s and my better days were behind me, but Bisping was a rising star in the MMA, Cage Warriors and Ultimate Fight Club scene, and probably the top guy in England at the time. He was unbeaten in his first five bouts and trained in a traditional form of jiu jitsu known as Yawara Ryu, as well as kick-boxing, and he was a big name in Knock Down Sport Budo when he was still in his teens. I never bothered to train in the martial arts; I relied on my natural fighting skills instead.

The fight, at the Xscape centre in Castleford, was an Ultimate Force promotion and the Cage Warriors light-heavyweight title was up for grabs. I should have known what I was up against: Bisping was the master craftsman, as hard as granite and sly as a fox. Before the fight he'd smeared Vaseline all over his body so I couldn't get a hold on him. He was as slippery as an eel and every time I tried to pin him down he'd wriggle out of my grasp. It was like trying to grapple with a giant bar of wet soap. And all the while he kept spiking me: landing elbows on my face as he pinned me to the ground. Then he'd pound me with his fists. He was giving me a right proper hiding.

In cage fighting it's literally about getting on top of your man, taking him to ground and forcing a submission. Either that or you're beating him so hard that the ref stops it, or the on-site doctor calls for a stoppage. The cage was Bisping's specialism and the better man won, but he knew he'd been in a scrap alright. In the changing rooms afterwards, as I was getting stripped off, he came up to me and said he didn't think I'd be able to take so much pain. I told him I had a reputation for being able to take extreme physical suffering.

Two months after my debut cage scrap, Bisping won the FX3 light-heavyweight title and held onto his Cage Warriors belt in a Strike Force 2 bout against Miika Mehmet. Meanwhile, I kept jumping into The Cage with all the big mixed-martial-arts names; real top guys such as Norman Paraisy. I took him on at a moment's notice too. I was in the crowd for an Ultimate Force cage-fighting show and three fighters pulled out, including Paraisy's opponent. They dragged me out of the crowd and asked if I wanted to fight him – I was in there like a shot. It was dubbed the 'The Battle of Waterloo'. I lost by a choke submission in four minutes and 53 seconds. The guy was throttling me. He's a tough boy, that Paraisy.

Another time I'd gone to watch my mate fight at the Doncaster Dome. I was in the changing rooms and there was Ian Rush, one of the best cage warriors in the business, shouting and swearing because his opponent hadn't shown up. I knew I was roughly the same weight as Rush – about 14st at the time - so I walked over and offered to fight him. I made the offer just one hour before the fight was due to start. Rush was stunned.

His manager came up to me and asked if I was sure about what I was getting myself into. I explained that I'd jumped out of the crowd once before to fight one of the best cage fighters around on my debut. I told him I'd had plenty of practice in the gym with guys such as Nasty Neil. He seemed satisfied by this and the fight was set, so I rushed out to the car and grabbed a pair of shorts from the back seat. I dashed back inside, got changed, and the next thing you know I'm live on Sky TV!

When the MC told the crowd I'd agreed to the fight at an hour's notice they went wild. I knew I'd have to put on a bit of a show after that introduction, so I let The Beast loose on Rush. He was an extremely powerful lad and kept pinning me to the ground every time I tried something new. I managed to turn him over but when I had him down it was hard to keep him there. I was dropping the spike on him and could feel my elbows sinking into his cheekbones. I heard one or two cracks but the lad had bottle and never winced. Rush was just too good on the ground so I stepped back and started laying kicks into him while he was in the horizontal position. But he'd just grab me by the calves and pull me down again. We were grappling on the floor and had our legs locked around each other, trying to gain the upper hand. I started driving my fists into his calves and managed to rear up a little, giving me time to catch him with three or four good punches to the chin, nose and temple. I ended up winning by a technical knock-out in four-and-a-half minutes. The crowd erupted. I was the big hero that night.

Little did I know, as I marched triumphantly out of the cage and jumped back in the car for the short drive back to Hemsworth, that just a few weeks later I would be the villain of the piece at a tribute night held in honour of one of the most successful fighters of all time.

11) The Court of King Joe

The Joe Calzhage Tribute Night bummed me out from the start. I was a special guest at the event but I didn't want to be there from the start: all that back-slapping just ain't my cup of tea. It was the Court of King Joe and I wanted no part of it.

Now I'm sure the Welshman was a great fighter, but, the thing is, I'd stopped watching boxing by the time he came on the scene and I'd never really seen him fight. He's probably one of the greatest super-middleweight champions there's ever been, but he could have been a back-street bum for all I cared. If truth be told, I plain didn't like the guy.

All his acolytes had turned up to pay their respects to the great man and take it in turns to say how wonderful he was. I was at the top table with Joe and his men. He'd just made his first speech and everybody was up on their feet roaring, clapping and shouting his name. Suddenly, out of this din came the shriek of a Nokia 636. An old Irish folk song was blasting out of my handset, piercing the rousing applause and bringing the room to a complete hush. Three hundred pairs of eyes were fixed on me as my hand desperately scrambled around my trouser pocket trying to get a hold of the damned phone. Because of the way I was sat, the pocket of my trousers was clinging to my leg and making it difficult to get the phone out. And still the Irish folk song kept ringing out.

I looked over at my daughter, Carla, who was in the audience. Her face had gone a kind of crimson red. Finally, I managed to wrench the phone out of my pocket. But, instead of turning it off and putting an end to the matter there and then, I answered it. It was my mate 'Grog' calling from Hemsworth. Now, instead of telling 'Grog' to call back later, as I would normally do, I started nattering to him on the phone, my thick Yorkshire vowels booming across the room.

"Hey up Grog! Yeah, I'll pick you up about four – no, make that seven. I should be about an hour. Alright son, no worries…"

Calzaghe's people were looking at me like I'd grown another head. I remember one of his guys actually looked like he was about to weep. I think if I'd have gotten up in the middle of Calzaghe's speech and pulled a moony at the bespectacled woman in the front row, the shock value wouldn't have been any less. The whole room fell silent. Their Messiah had just delivered his sermon and there was me arranging a night out in Hemsworth with Grog!

I looked over at Carla again. Her face had turned a kind of tomato red by now. Her jaw was almost touching the floor. She sent me a text which read: "What is wrong with you?!?"

I sent one back saying: "I want to get down!"

Another text winged back to me: "Stay where you are!"

I did stay put but I bet Carla wishes now that I'd have got the hell out of there because what happened next turned her face from crimson to ashen. Calzaghe's courtiers passed me the microphone to say a few complimentary words about the 'champ'. What they actually got was something completely off the script, so jaw-droppingly outrageous that I swear I saw one of Joe's guys nearly choke on his vol-au-vent. Here's how it went: I got to my feet and mumbled a few run-of-the-mill things about boxing and the noble art. The audience wasn't entirely impressed at this point, but at least they weren't grossly offended. But then Joe's boys tried to cajole me into licking their man's backside – BAD MOVE. They asked me what I remembered about Joe and his magnificent career. That's when I delivered the sucker punch. It was so entirely unexpected and came as such an earth-shattering blow to Calzaghe and his crew that the entire room was frozen in silence again. First I paused for dramatic effect, clearing my throat and looking for all the word like I was about to deliver a fitting eulogy to the Great Man. Then, looking right into the bowels of the crowd, I delivered this corker: "I can't really say much about Joe because I've never seen him fight."

Well, you could have heard a pin drop. I looked into the audience and saw a lot of big, sturdy fellas looking like they were about to get up and lamp me one. I could see veins popping out of their heads, their fists clench.

That night in Doncaster, I knew what it was like to be roundly hated. Those people thought I had disrespected a great man. I would have loved to have told them what I really thought of him! Instead, I kept my mouth shut and did one. Carla told me afterwards that she thought she was seeing things. She said it was one of the most embarrassing moments of her life. Oh daddy, what have you done?!

I'll never forget Calzaghe's face that night - he was absolutely livid. In fact, we nearly came to blows at one point. It happened just before we were about to go on stage. We had a little set-to and, though I don't want to go into any detail here, suffice to say it ended with me saying "on the end of your cock". Then the compere announced my name and I walked on stage. Time to go, boys and girls!

Don't think for a minute I didn't realise my behaviour that night was shameful. No matter how much I disliked Calzaghe, it was bad manners to say the least and I should have known better. It was so unlike me to be that rude but maybe, in my subconscious, I was trying to piss off the Calzaghe crew and ruin their party. I do pride myself on being a gentleman so I have to say it was bang out of order. That said, me and my mates did have a good old chuckle about it afterwards and, if nothing else, it did brighten up a dull evening!

A few days later I received some news which put an even bigger smile on my face. I was told by a bare-knuckle fixer that he'd arranged for me to fight the Leicester Bulldog on his own patch. I was elated: The Bulldog was renowned as a proper terror merchant; a grunting, snorting, foul-tempered beast of a man who might have the power to put me away. I couldn't wait for the hour to arrive.

12) Bulldog

The alarm shrieked. It shook me out of a deep slumber - the day had arrived.

I'd waited so long for this: so many weeks up at the crack of dawn, endless months in the gym to get my medicine. Everything had been geared towards this day.

I was 42 now but felt like I was in the prime of my life - I must whip the Dog. I rang the lads up and had a kiss and a cuddle with the missus. She wished me luck.

I went to pick Mark up. We gave each other the nod – we were in for a good day.

We jumped in the motor and drove through the village to get Neil. He and Mark were handy with their fists and good on the ground. Not that we were going to have any trouble, but people can fall out. Paul, the fixer, gave me his word: it would be a fair fight. I knew everything would be ok.

We talked in the car as we drove down to the gym; we were all on form. We arrived at George's house. He'd been to lots of my fights, had George - some with gloves, others with the fists. This was just a walk in the park for Georgie boy.

We all went inside to see his new-born baby girl, Honey, and I gave her a good-luck kiss. I had a look at George's fish pond, then we jumped in the Range Rover and headed off to meet the Leicester Bull Dog on his own turf.

George was driving. I was sat in the front passenger seat clenching my fists so tight they were beginning to ache. All we knew was that the fight would be held in a cow field on a farm somewhere in Leicester. It was set for two o'clock. The fixers called it 'The Battle Amongst the Cattle'.

On the way down I kept thinking about a film I'd watched a few days earlier. It was called 'The Big Fight: The Mystery Man against the Leicester Bulldog'. It was about The Dog's last fight. Paul had made it and gave me a copy when he came to interview me at the gym. I watched it at my mate Butch's house. The fight lasted six minutes – The Bulldog won. He broke his hand in the fight and needed time to recover before he met me – we gave him six months.

The Bulldog's knuckle record was five fights and five wins. He was 18st and 5ft 10; a man mountain with a fearsome reputation and a short fuse. I was 14st, but I had given Butch the nod to speak to Paul and get it on. I had come across men like this before.

We met Paul on the way down to Leicester. He was with two cameramen who seemed like nice enough fellas, but I could tell from the way they were looking at me that they were expecting something bigger. I just knew they thought I was in for a pasting.

We followed Paul's car for maybe 10 miles down little country roads, then pulled into an old farm yard. There were three or four guys there taking photos and one with a video camera. We all shook hands then walked through the yard into an old barn to get changed. I put my jeans on: I wanted to fight in trousers; it's more comfortable.

The barn was grim. There were old hammers and axes everywhere; big old farm tools on the walls and machinery scattered about. It was sort of primeval.

"Jesus, what are we doing here?" I said to the lads.

We were taken through a second door into another room, done out like an old pub. There were tables, chairs and a bar in the shape of a half-moon. Photos of old bare-knuckle fighters were hung up on the walls. In the top corner of the room was a swallow's nest where three chicks were chirping away.We all shook the barman's hand; he was the guy who owned the farm. This was the place where we were going to have a drink after the fight.

The farm wasn't a pretty sight. The farmer had put his cattle away but there was cow shit all over the place and big heaps of horse crap everywhere. Paul took us through the yard where two big dogs were barking away. We made our way into the cow field and saw the ring. The perimeter was marked by four, seven-foot posts bashed three-and-a-half feet into the ground. They had tied two big ropes around the posts to make the ring.

The referee came over. Paul introduced us: "This is Dave

Radford."

We gave him the nod and shook hands. The ref explained the rules: "No biting, no holding; I want fair play."

Fair play in the knuckle game is doing as you're told, sticking to the rules. No dirty tricks; a good, clean fight.

There was a good dozen fellows stood around the video camera on a tripod and the filming had already begun. Paul introduced me to David Platts, Bulldog's corner man and trainer who was affectionately known as 'Leicester's notorious poacher'. He was 6ft 7in and wore a long, black trench coat and trilby hat. Butch had told me a lot about Mr Platts: he bought and sold lurchers and did a bit of this and that.

"How's the ring?" he said. "Is it okay for you lads?"

We gave him the nod.

There were seven or eight men stood around in trench coats and flat caps. The referee had an old pair of boots on with his trousers tucked into his socks and his shirt sleeves rolled up. He was wearing a pair of braces holding his trousers up and had a trilby hat perched on his head. Jesus, he looked a right sight!

Our lads felt out of place. They were surrounded by Ronny and Reggie Kray lookalikes, so they marched off to get a couple of dusty long coats from the barn. Meanwhile, there was still no sign of the Dog. One of the cameramen who had seen him fight said to me: "He's a lot bigger than you; move around him, make him tired, keep out of his way."

I gave him the nod but inside I was thinking that the Bulldog had better keep out of *my* way: I had seen the ring, the crowd was okay and the lads were nice and calm. I was ready.

That said, it's hard to keep a serious face when your mates are striding across a dung-spattered cow field in big black trench coats and wearing ridiculous hats. Neil and Mark had somehow managed to find these dusty old rags in a barn where rats were scurrying about all over the place.

They were itching like mad because of all the dust and cobwebs on the trench coats. They looked like something out of the Fantastic Four! Everyone was laughing like hyenas - even the Ronnie Kray lookalikes. Then the laughing stopped and me and the boys moved away from the crowd - we didn't want to get too friendly with the others. They were nice people but they were there to see me get a hiding. I knew this was going to be a tough one. There are no easy fights; you just take the rough with the smooth. I heard one of their crowd say that the Bulldog was up for it and he was in a very bad mood. They said he hadn't wanted to talk to anyone, just wanted to get inside the ring and fight. Then someone said he was here. We looked around and there he was. He didn't come straight across; he went up to the top of the field and back again, then came bounding towards the ring.

One of his men said: "He's on the warpath; he's really mad."

I turned to the ref and said if he came anywhere near me I'd start fighting straight away – I take no chances.

"Okay, I'll tell him."

The poor ref; he was scared stiff. I'd told him earlier that he should stay on the outside of the ring: it was too small for three men.

"You might get hit," I joshed.

He went up the field to meet the Dog. I heard him say: "No holding, no head-butting, no gouging."

Then I started to get that old feeling, that lovely tingle down the spine. The adrenaline buzz before a fight is so irresistible it's hard to explain. I looked at the lads and they gave me the nod. George kept telling me to take it easy.

"Let's have a look at him first; use that jab, move off him."

Neil and Mark chipped in: "You know what to do and you can do it."

I took my shirt off and stepped into the ring. There was no canvas on the ground, just grass. No cow shit, but, boy, could you smell it.

The Bulldog was still on his way down; I could hear him grunting. I'd heard about this before, the way he tried to scare the bejesus out of his opponents before they stepped into the ring. All I could think was, 'if he slips on some cow shit on the way down, I won't be able to fight him for laughing'.

I looked over at this snarling giant in jeans as he came striding over. He was still grunting and steam was coming off him as if he were on fire. His friends gave me a knowing look - they were smirking. My boys gave me the nod. A man will fight all day in front of his friends, but take those friends away and he's only half the fighter.

The Bulldog did as he was told when he got inside the ring. He stayed in his corner as the ref mumbled stuff to him: none of this and none of that, and keep your fingers out of his eyes. The ref was so nervous he ended up saying, "this is a two-minute round with a one-minute fight", which puzzled the timekeeper and confused the hell out of the rest of us.

It was to be a straight, stand-up fight – no biting, butting, holding or elbowing. If a man goes down, stand off him; if he's okay and wants to continue, let him up and carry on. If the man has had enough, the fight's over.

I touched fists with the lads; I could hardly look at Mark and Neil and keep a straight face. But it was the timekeeper who had us in stitches. He was holding a frying pan and gave it a belt with a stick: 'Bingggg!' Show time.

Knuckle fights don't have time limits – you fight until one of the fighters has had enough. Fights have been known to last for several hours. They are usually held in grass fields or on gravel, but hardly ever in rings. It wasn't my idea to fight between the ropes but it suited me fine. Paul had wanted the fight in the ring so he could film it better. He wanted two-minute rounds with a one-minute rest between each. It was also agreed that neither me nor the Dog would wear our tops for the 'no- holding-and-hitting' reason.

We met in the centre of the ring and stood there toe-to-toe for about five seconds, trading big, heavy blows. He landed a big right hook right on the end of my chin; it stunned me and sent me sprawling backwards. We went back in at each other; the Bulldog was growling. He was untidy - we knew he would be, but he was a lot quicker than we thought. We were both landing good, clean shots, but I couldn't get him bang on the chin because his arms were so big I couldn't get through. That big, bald head was out of range and he tucked his chin in well.

I kept pushing forward but he was landing big rights on the top of my forehead. One of them split my head right open; it left a huge gash two inches long and an inch wide. My left eye was choked with blood; I kept wiping it out but the blood kept spurting out. I was fighting with one eye.

I moved off him and sent in some big right hands to the body. He just smiled, but I knew they'd hurt him. We slugged it out again and ended up in the corner. I slipped down to my right and sent three big hooks into his body. He stepped back and didn't smile this time.

I remember thinking how brutal this fight must have looked from the outside. The shots were cracking on the side of our skulls and arms like whiplashes. We were cut so badly it looked like someone had chucked a bucket of blood over us.

WHAM!

He sent me wobbling again with another clean shot to the chin. I blanked out for half a second but came back with a good long jab. I stood off him again, landing some lovely, long jabs as the blood oozed out of my cut. I threw a right hook which hit him right on the side of the head. The punch was so hard I could feel my knuckles sink into his skull - but he didn't go down. His neck was so big and his body so strong.

The thought went through my mind that this guy was not going to fold. Then the timekeeper hit the frying pan with the stick: "Time lads."

The first round was up and I was already soaked in blood. As I went to my corner, George was working on my cut. Then the timekeeper told us to get ready.

"Come on lads!" cried the ref.

I heard the Dog growl: "Has he come to fight or what?"

I immediately pulled away from George. You see, what
the Bulldog said was a good sign for me. When a man starts
complaining during a fight there is definitely something
bothering him – he's not happy. I was ready. This was what
I loved doing the most. This was my heaven. Sometimes you
don't ever want the fight to stop. All the memories from my
fights are golden memories.

You could hear the crunching of bones as we went
straight back in at each other. The Bulldog was snarling
again but I kept him in range, working off the jab. We
moved around each other, letting the shots go. I stepped to
my side and hit him with a lovely left hook on the chin. His
legs went from underneath him; he was flat out. The referee
was straight in: "Get back!"

I gave the Dog some distance: I didn't want to destroy
him, I wanted to trade blows. I waited in my corner and
looked over at him - he was still down. He wasn't moving
and had his hands over his eyes. George shouted: "He's had
enough referee."

The ref was having none of it: "I'm the referee! I'll decide
if he's had enough."

Then he turned to the Bulldog: "Are you okay Tony; do
you want to carry on?"

The ref gave him a bit of time to come round, which was
fair play.

The lads were bursting with adrenaline, their fists tight
and teeth glued together. I was in my own little zone, just
waiting to get the job done. The Bulldog got back to his feet;
he had a cut on his right eyelid. I thought, 'you fool'.

"Are you okay Tony?" asked the ref.

"Just give me five minutes," said the Dog.

"No, you fight now or it will be stopped."

The lads gave me the nod and we went back to business.
The Dog came at me with both fists, aiming for my cut,
which hadn't stopped bleeding. The ring was now a blood
bath.

I took some more big shots off him. He was a game fighter with a big heart, but then I sent in a left hook which knocked him sideways and put him back on the defensive. That's when I noticed the cut over his eye. His cheeks were bruised and puffy - I ripped into them mercilessly.

The Bull was starting to snort now; his breathing was laboured and he was huffing and puffing. I sensed it was time for the kill. The final blow was a lovely right hand over the top. The ref jumped in as the Bulldog fell to the ground, out cold. He stood over the Dog's huge frame: "That's it; he's finished. No more."

George climbed through the ropes and came running over to me with a towel, which he put over the cut that was still gushing with blood.

"Great fight Dave; too strong for him. No-one can take shots like that; something had to give."

There are two ways to take a good punch: you can take one then coward away, or you can take it and come back with one twice as hard. But there are some punches you just can't take. If you get hit on the button, you're going down – every man has a button.

The ref came over and raised my hand: "I'm the referee and I've stopped the fight – this man is the winner."

Everyone round the ring was clapping. I went over to The Bulldog; he was still unconscious, lying on his back. I knelt down beside him as Jim Woolly, one of his corner men, put a wet towel over his head.

"Hello Tony, are you okay?" I said.

He started to come round a bit, grunting like a dog. He was still bleeding from the eye.

"Good fight Tony; you're a quick man for your size. No hard feelings."

I went over to his crowd; they couldn't wait to shake my hand. Then I climbed through the ropes. Paul was standing there.

"Jesus Dave, that was some fight. I've seen some fights but that was a corker."

Everyone was shaking hands, everybody was happy -

even the Bulldog's crowd. They'd seen their man get beat but it was one of those fights they'd never forget. It was a gentlemen's fight; a straight, stand-up bout. George and the Dog's two corner men helped him to his feet. He was okay now; he'd come round. He came over to me. I said I was sorry – a daft thing to say.

"Don't be sorry, I would have done the same to you," he snorted.

George came over: "You should have seen it, Dave, from out here; there were some big bombs thrown in there. I thought someone was going down in the first round. Something had to give; the noises from the shots were brutal."

We made our way across the field, dodging the cow shit, talking about the fight. I heard Mr Platts say: "That man will take some beating."

I felt great. Truth is: I would have felt great even if I'd have lost, as long as I'd enjoyed it – that's all that matters to me.

We got back to the car and the first-aid box came out. The cut was deep and very wide. It needed stitches but we couldn't stop the blood flowing. We decided to treat it when we got back home.

Joe Woolly and the Dog suddenly chipped up; they asked us to look at his cut. Me and George cleaned it up for him and put some strips on. Joe said: "Look at this; this is what it's all about – you've just had a big battle out there and you're helping him with the cut."

A man who goes into battle and has no hard feelings whether he wins or loses is a good man; so too he who loves the game, needs to fight, but is no bully.

Once we had sorted the Dog's cuts, I rang Butch, who was down at the yard with the horses.

"Butch, I beat him; I knocked him out in the second round."

"Dave, I didn't think you'd knock him out," he said. "You've done well; I'll tell the boys to spread the word around."

We all went up to the barn for a drink and to talk about the fight. I was asked lots of questions: how many street fights had I had? How many cage fights? How many boxing matches? These were genuine people who had a lot respect for us, and we had a lot of respect for them. I talked to them about the Roberto Duran fight in South Africa; I thought they must have known about that. The Dog's men told me that, before the fight, they had asked for a picture of me, which Paul had given to them. They said I looked different in the photo to how I looked in the flesh. I could have told them that you can't go on the look of a photo; that's not going to tell you whether a man will win or lose. It's not the size of the man that counts, it's the size of the man's heart.

Paul told me to come outside and talk about the fight in front of the cameras. He said he had another fight in mind and would I be interested? I said my bit then went back to join the lads. We stayed for another drink, shook hands with the others and cleaned the shit off our shoes. Then we got in the car and drove back home. On the way back we were all making calls to give our friends the news that The Bulldog had been beaten. We called in the local for one, raised our glasses and gave the nod.

13) I Am Jehovah

I was the toast of the village again after defeating the Bulldog. Hemsworth's a hard town but the people are good judges of character and will respect a good man. You get poverty and warmth in equal measure in our neck of the woods.

There are two sides to the town, of course. It's plagued by the same mindless violence you see in every town and city on a Saturday night. There are plenty of tough nuts down our way – we're bred hard – but I've never had any problems with the bovver boys. At least, nothing I've not been able to resolve with a quiet word, allied to a strong fist if necessary. But there are times when violence is the only option. It's my back-up policy but not one I like to use if I can help it. Sometimes it's inescapable.

If people are silly enough and drunk enough to have a go in the pub, I don't blink but tell them to leave it; get yourself home and sober up. I'm so meek and mild in these situations they probably think that's the end of it; perhaps they have a good laugh at me with their mates when my back is turned. Maybe they think I'm a pussy. That's fine with me; I can sleep easy on that.

The next day, depending on who was doing the mouthing, I might pay them a visit – alone, of course, except for my good buddies Jo and Herbert. I go round without warning to the guy's house and knock on his door. Perhaps he thinks it's the postman with a surprise package; maybe it's the milkman come for his money. It can't be the Jehovah's Witnesses – it's far too early for them. So who on earth could that be, dear, on our front doorstep at this hour? Why, it's the friendly neighbourhood beast! Only this time he's not smiling - and he's certainly not come for your empties. Here stands Jehovah and he's gonna blast you out of existence!

The look of astonishment on their faces soon turns to horror when they realise why I'm there. The smug grin is gone, the cockiness and bravado of the night before evaporate in an instant. They're snookered and they know it. Some of them visibly shake. It's the nightmare scenario and there's no way out. They're on their own now; no mates to back them up and no audience to play up to. Some of them try pleading, but they're shitting themselves so much they stammer and end up tongue-tied. No words are gonna help you now son – you made your mistake last night and now you must pay.

I stand there unmoved, completely expressionless. The words are delivered slowly, crisply, coldly: "You've got to fight me now you are sober. You spoilt my night; come out here and fight or I'll put you away now."

Some people simply need disciplining. They get drunk and think they have the strength of 10 men. They think they're Rocky Balboa all of a sudden and, with all that booze inside them, they're ready to take on anyone. I was once in a pub in Ryhill, a town not far from ours. I was minding my own business, choosing some songs from the juke box, when a guy swung for me with a pool cue. The pool table was right next to the juke box and he must have thought I was getting in his way because I felt a pool cue poke me in the back a few times. I turned round and told him he'd be picking up his teeth with broken fingers if he carried on, but carry on he did. The silly boy was holding the cue like a baseball bat and swung for my head. I ducked out of the way and landed an absolute haymaker right in his mug. I'd caught him just as he was off-balance - he went down like a stack of cards. Then I knelt on him and drove another couple of punches into his head for good measure. One of them landed straight in the temple and cleaned him out.

I don't like hurting people but this guy just had to be disciplined. I'd given him a warning but he still kept on coming, so he had to be punished. It takes a lot for me to go, but when someone's swinging a pool cue at you for no good reason, that person has to accept he's out of line and deserves a beating. People can take the piss out of me all they want; I've got a pretty high tolerance level and I let most things go. But there are people who take things that little bit too far and need disciplining. If, when I'm out at night, I get the tiniest scent of menace in the air and any of my family are around, I have to deal with the situation in hand. It's at times like this when The Beast is completely unrestrained.

As a case in point, let me to tell you the story about the three blokes from Fitzwilliam, the village next to ours, who came into our local pub causing some bother. They came into the tap room where I was having a drink with the missus. I could sense they were on the warpath and my hunch came true when they attacked a guy who was on his own - I had to act. I put my pint down and calmly walked over to where the three thugs were giving the guy a hammering. I sorted them out good style – brayed the three of them twice over. I was arrested and given an 18-month suspended prison sentence. I was lucky: the courts were in mind to send me straight to the slammer for six months.

I'd do bird no problem if it meant my family stayed out of harm's way. Our family is tight - very tight. If one of us is cut then we all bleed.

14) Gareth

My beloved nephew hanged himself at the age of 21 – it broke my heart. What a terrible waste of a young life.

We were closer than brothers. He was my soul mate, best friend. Gareth had so much self-doubt and no self-esteem. And yet he was handsome, charming and full of life. He was just a lovely human being who the ladies adored and the men respected, but, Gareth being Gareth, he never believed it. He thought he was worthless, a stain on mankind when in fact he was one of its brightest stars.

He fractured his eye when he was young which caused one of his eyes to close up permanently. It made him really self-conscious. In the pub, when everyone else was having a good time, he would analyse himself, question every little thing in his life in minute detail. If something was bothering him he just couldn't let it go; he'd gnaw on it like a dog with a bone. It was such a terrible shame. I loved him like I loved my mother, but they both went away.

Maybe there are some people who are just wired up to take their own lives. Perhaps there are those who don't see themselves as others see them. Gareth's dad took his own life too - he shot himself.

People didn't think of our Gareth as a depressive person because he was one of those who could hide his emotions from all but those who were closest to him. He had a huge heart but went into depth about absolutely everything. Apparently – and I didn't know this at the time – he'd been threatening to take his own life for quite some time. Evidently he'd told his mam. Somebody later told me he'd actually tried to commit suicide once before.

He was a very religious person. He had his bible which he read over and over, and he used to quote extracts from it. He knew I was an atheist but never brought me up on it and never talked to me about his beliefs. I suppose some people just have no luck and that was our Gareth. He'd been bullied at school and used to get terrible headaches caused by a build-up of fluid on his brain. When I go in for a fight I can feel Gareth right there beside me. I have a 'chat' with him before the bell goes and, afterwards, whether I win or lose, I dedicate the fight to him. Maybe the reason I felt so close to him was that, deep down, we were both haunted by the same demons. I wouldn't say that I had a dark soul but when the Black Dog appears I can get very low. Maybe I'm depressed now. Perhaps that's why I continue to fight though my best years are behind me. Maybe that's why I continue to get my head bashed in. Am I punishing myself for Gareth killing himself? Am I blaming myself for the loss of my mother?

I know exactly what it's like to be down there in the pit, believe me. After Gareth died I was knee deep in the trough, as low as you could get. Dark thoughts filled my every waking moment. I couldn't even get up off the settee and when I did manage to get up I'd just drift aimlessly around the house like a ghost with no-one to haunt. I must have been hell to live with at the time. I even took time off work and anybody who knows me well enough will tell you that's unheard of with me. It's hard to do anything – and that includes moving – when everything is black and there's not a single ray of light on your horizon.

The doctor gave me anti-depressants but all they did was knock me out. And I was out for a long, long time. I was taking three 50mg Tramadol tablets a day. They had given me the wrong dose, double the strength I should have been on. Yeah, I was pretty gaga in those days.

15) The Claw

Nobody's ever put me down in sparring - not even The Nasty One - but Craig 'The Clobberer' Smith has come mighty close. He's my favourite sparring partner inside the ring and owns one of the deadliest punches I've ever come across. I call it The Claw.

It's a left hook that starts at the hips and shoots up through his upper torso like a piston. When you get hit by The Claw the shockwaves reverberate through your entire body. Your skull rattles, your central nervous system momentarily closes down. It's an incredible punch and Craig has the patent on it. I remember once he banged me so hard I was out on my feet. It was a Claw punch, one that only he can throw. My lights went out. I was seeing stars but I carried on. It was just like when I fought Duran: my mind must have been telling my legs to go down, but they refused to buckle. I drifted back into consciousness for a millisecond and then: BOOM! The Clobberer caught me with another haymaker and I was out on my feet again for about a second. I was bobbing in and out of reality and still fighting.

Craig is one of four regular sparring partners I train with at the gym. They're all game lads with plenty of heart – it's like fighting my reflection. I'm never short of a good sparring partner who knows how to dispense an adequate dose of medicine. If Craig's not available, I know there are at least three other lads who are just at the end of the phone, ready to nip down to the club at a moment's notice. Sometimes, when we're really in need of a dose, we'll go down in the cellar below the gym for a no-holds-barred session. It's like something out of Fight Club and we can't live without it.

Virtually every time I fight The Clobberer he busts my nose and I come out of the gym looking like I've been swimming in blood. I walk down to the Alpha Club below with my face caked in the stuff, my vest stuck to my chest by the sticky red glue. The fellas in the club don't bat an eyelid; they've seen it all before. It wouldn't be Sunday lunchtime if they didn't see me coming downstairs bloodied up to the eyes. It makes me feel like I've earned a pint.

It's quite easy to bust my nose nowadays: it's just like turning on a tap. One or two good jabs from The Clobberer is usually all it takes for the floodgates to open. It's like a red waterfall that paints the canvas red.

There's a sign above my training ring which says: 'Blood is only red sweat.' It's there to remind me and the other guys that, no matter how much blood is split in sparring, it's worth every drop.

It's like preaching to the converted with The Clobberer: he can scent blood. Sometimes he'll play cat-and-mouse with me and deliberately avoid my pecker – but I know it's only a matter of time before he lands a big one on the snout. Sometimes I'll egg him on: "You've not got my nose yet Craig. I haven't even got a nose bleed!"

Pop! Pop! Pop!

I love getting drenched in the red stuff because then I know I've had a good workout. I lose more blood than most boxers mainly because my nose is so susceptible now. There's no other choice when I'm sparring with Craig: he's the expert nose-popper and I couldn't wish for a nicer guy to rearrange my snout on a Sunday morning.

My beak has taken some good hammerings down the years. I think it's because I've got a very upright style of fighting. I stand tall, go straight down the middle and I'm always on the front foot. This means I'm walking into plenty of jabs to the nose, which is fine with me.

I've got one of those classic boxing veterans' faces now: there's certainly no doubting my occupation when people first meet me. I'm not as pretty as I used to be and I'm certainly no Calzaghe, who seems to have come through the fight game pretty much unscathed. If you didn't know who he was, you wouldn't look at him and think he was a boxer, would you? With me, it's practically written on my face. Never mind: I see it as the fruit of my toils, the warrior's scars. Besides, my eyes still see and the nose is not there to look pretty – it's there to do a job. It's a working nose and it's put in some bloody good hours down the years. When the time comes it will have earned its retirement – but not just yet.

Top left: Me and me Mam
Top right: The Beast as a teenage fighter. Wasn't I a handsome devil!

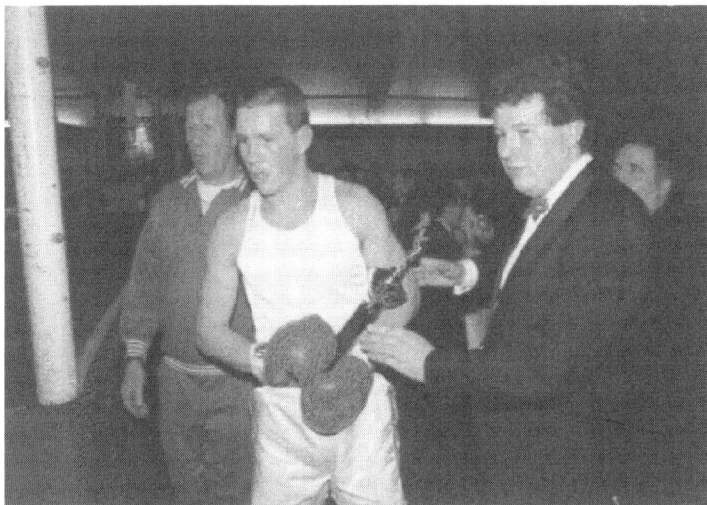

Me and my dad (left) after one of my junior fights. Don't ask me who the geezer presenting the trophy is - my memory's not that good!

Grappling on the floor with cage fiend Norman Paraisy. July 21, 2007.

Top left: Squaring up with The Bulldog in front of the eccentric referee in mad clothes.
Bottom left: Unleashing the first pile-driver to floor The Bulldog . Top right:
Crouching down beside The Dog after the second knock-down finishes the contest.
Bottom right: Me and Bulldog outside the barn after the 'Battle Amongst the Cattle'.

Me with Duran and my trainer James Walker after the fight in South Africa - the hardest one of my life.

Going toe-to-toe with The Bulldog during our blood-spattered encounter in 2009.

Me and Duran square up for the cameras during a speaking engagement in Doncaster.

Me and our Gareth when he was a nipper, bless him.

Fists up with Mr Platts, 'Leicester's notorious poacher'.

Me with the belt that Duran sent me after our fight in Africa. He wrote a message on it which said: 'To Dave, you hurt me in Africa.' It's one of my most treasured possessions.

83

Battling with Roberto 'Hands of Stone' Duran in the sweltering African heat in 1997. He gave me such a beating in those last few rounds that I had to have a hernia operation afterwards.

At a sportsmen's dinner with the great Marvin Hagler and (left) James Walker.

The Clobberer catches me with a good 'un at the Alpha gym. We don't half love our Sunday morning sessions.

Our Gareth: I loved him like a son.

Poor old Billy Goat copped a beauty off the beast.

Friends reunited: Me, Screaming Skull and the Hands of Stone during a sportsmen's dinner at the Alpha Club in Hemsworth.

'Smokin Joe' Frazier at my new gym above the Alpha Club in May 2011. He died six months later..

The Beast on a work site circa 1996.

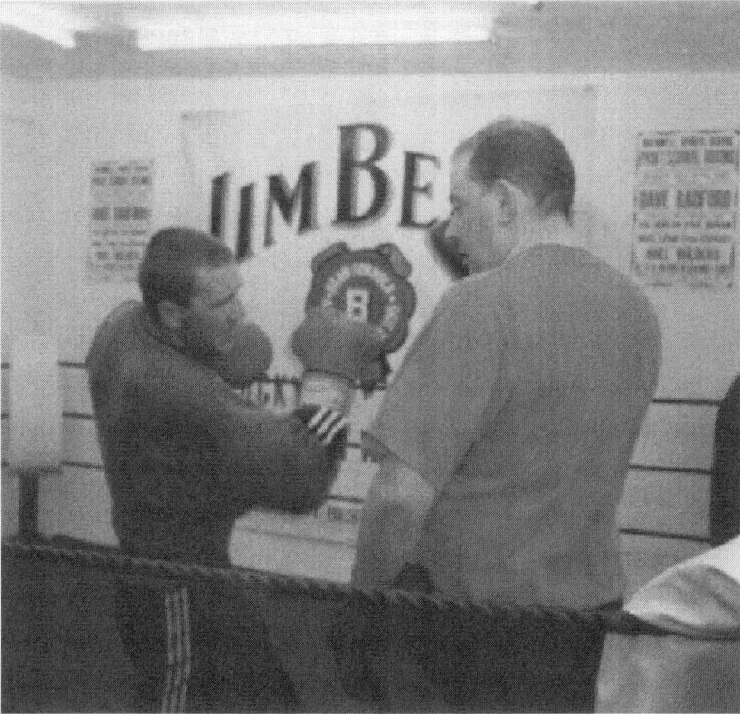

Pounding the pads with trainer James Walker in my prime.

Me and my old mate Pete Wiggins when we were spring chickens.

I must stop meeting up with old Stone Hands - it brings back bad memories! Here we are with Roberto junior (second from left), my Becky and Carla.

Me (background) looking like a blood-soaked mummy during my fight with The Bulldog in a cow field in Leicester. In the foreground is the weirdest-dressed ref in the world.

The Court of King Joe: Calzhage (far left) delivers a speech to his fawning fans at Skellow Grange, Doncaster, during his tribute night. At the top table (from left) are the MC for the night, Joe's dad Enzo, Calzhage's corner man and, last but not least, The Beast.

16)   The Elephant Man

For someone like me, it's hard to think about retirement when you're being tempted into fight after fight by the bare-knuckle fixers. My mobile seems to be constantly buzzing nowadays with offers of a dust-up.

It only takes a few phone-calls to get a cobble fight on, but where you'll be fighting is anyone's guess. It might be a dingy bar, a field full of cow shit, a dank cellar or an old warehouse.

I fought 'wonder kid' Danny Draper in a hell-hole of a bar in Leicester on April 29, 2012. Boy, what a crap-house that was. Not the kind of place you'd want to take the missus on a Saturday night. I hate bare-knuckling on anything but grass. You see, when my opponent goes down – and go down he surely must if The Beast is on his mettle - I don't want to be worrying about him banging his head on the hard surface. If he does, he could end up very poorly and you could be facing six or seven years inside.

There are no laws to protect you on the knuckle scene: it's unlicensed and therefore still illegal as things stand. So, if you seriously hurt someone and the Boys in Blue get wind of it, it would be no different to badly injuring someone in a street fight or in the pub. It really is time they brought this thing out into the open. Let's have it staged in pubs with a proper licence so everyone can watch it. Only that way will you remove the perceived seediness from the sport. Bare knuckle is how it was in the beginning and, as far as I'm concerned, it's how it should be. It's the purest form of the sport and as old as the hills.

What you have today is a middle man who gets the fight on in secret and tries to keep the long arm of the law at bay. For the Draper fight, it was simply a guy who happened to have my phone number. His name is Andy Topliffe, a former knuckler who had to pack it in after a gunman pumped him full of lead. Andy turned to promoting BKB fights under B-Bad Promotions and now he's trying to make the sport more legitimate. He's already brought the BKB

British title belt back into existence for the first time since 1890 and now he's on with a new project called Field Rage, where you have a doctor on the scene and an ambulance at the ready in case one of the fighters gets seriously injured. He's trying to make it more mainstream like MMA cage-fighting, which is much more brutal. Good luck to him – I hope he pulls it off for the sport's sake.

I'd met Andy just once in a pub. It was one of those situations where he knew me but I didn't know him. All I knew was that he arranged field fights - that's when my ears pricked up. He called me and asked if I fancied a knuckle fight in B-Bad 1, the first in a series of BKB shows which were meant to bring the sport out into the open. I liked Andy and I'm always up for a fight, so I said yes.

I was supposed to be fighting a guy called Jeff Sutton, a big bruiser - 6ft 8-plus. I knew if I took him on I'd get smashed up, win or lose. However, my main concern, as usual, was working out how to tell the missus that I'd be coming home in a mess again. She hates me fighting, especially bare-knuckle. But as it turned out, the fight against The Bruiser didn't happen. I was to fight gipsy boy Draper instead.

Andy said to me that the giant I was supposed to be fighting had seen me going at it with The Bulldog on Youtube and didn't want any of that, thank you very much. He'd also heard I'd fought Duran. According to Andy, Sutton had been shouting and swearing at him down the phone, saying there was no way he was fighting Dave Radford. Running out of options, Andy asked Draper if he wanted to fight and he said "no problem". Draper knew I'd fought Duran and he knew I'd been in the ring with The Dog. He was also aware that I'd been in the cage - I had to give this man respect.

Somebody told me later that he'd had two bare-knuckles and won them both, plus loads of unlicensed bouts. At least I knew a bit about the guy. Normally, I go into a fight knowing next to nothing about my opponent. On the knuckle scene you're often fighting guys you've never heard of.

They might be complete nut jobs for all you know. It's all the same to me: I just put in a bit of training and hope for the best.

Sometimes your man doesn't turn up, which means you end up fighting someone else who's filling in for him at the last minute. In these situations, you don't have a clue what you're coming up against. You could have a bear, a lion or a mouse in front of you. It's pot luck and just adds to the danger factor.

But this guy Draper knew exactly what he would be up against and didn't seem in the least bit fazed. It has to be said, though, that as good as he thought he was, he must have known he would be grappling with a Grizzly.

At 26, he was 16 years younger than me. I knew I would need to train hard but ended up putting in just three weeks at the gym. Apart from that, I did a few little runs, no more than two miles each. I sparred with The Clobberer a few times and he broke the side of my nose again. My poor old snout has taken a right bashing from The Clobberer down the years. You've got to admire the man for accuracy. When I chew my food nowadays I can hear my nose click - Craig always delivers the goods. I always give back just as good in return, of course. During our spars before the Draper fight, I hit him with Joseph and knocked his jaw from one side of his face to the other. The next day he could hardly eat his breakfast. He broke my nose and I caved his jaw in - it was a good couple of sessions.

I'd put on a bit of timber in the months leading up to the Draper fight and, to be honest, I wasn't fit enough. It was supposed to be 45-minute rounds with 10-minute rests in between - bollocks to that. I said to Andy that if you couldn't smash a man up in 10 minutes, break his fists or his cheekbones, you might as well not be in the game. If the beating was dished out correctly, a man could not absorb that amount of punishment for more than 10 minutes, not without the gloves on. Some can do it, don't get me wrong. They'll fight for an hour, maybe longer, but they always finish up with a busted nose, black eyes. When you're punching somebody so hard, for that long, that you're breaking their ribs, that's when the sport becomes dangerous. I've fought a few times with broken ribs and it's not pleasant. You can't pull in air: there's no way you can fight like that for an hour. And once you stop for 10 minutes, as they had planned for the Draper match, there's simply no way you can carry on. Your body goes into recovery mode and you start aching - you should not be fighting.

To be frank, I only had 10 minutes in me for the Draper fight anyway, but I didn't tell them that. I knew I would have to go for the jugular right from the off against the younger man. I needed to hurt him very badly and very quickly. If he was a dancer, let him catch me. Let him think he's hurt me; he'll keep coming in - then he's in the danger zone. That's when I bring old Joseph and Herbert out - those two never let me down.

As always, I took my band of closest friends along with me to the fight. We turned up in a Range Rover: me, The Clobberer, Screaming Skull, The Undertaker, Psycho, Nasty Neil and The Bull. Imagine having that lot round at your mother's for tea!

We got out of the Rover just outside the club, where a dozen shady-looking guys milling around a few old travellers' vans were putting the stare on us, smoking fags. They glowered but said nothing, so we carried on our way up to the entrance. I was feeling a bit edgy, not because I was worried about the outcome of the fight, but because I was convinced that my man wouldn't show. That's the way it is in the knuckle game: you prep yourself for months and get yourself all geared up knowing that your opponent might not turn up. I can understand, in a way, why some guys don't show up because you're fighting in places that are completely alien to you. Quite frankly, some bare-knuckle venues are downright scary and this was one of the worst I'd seen.

There are some so-called fighters who simply bottle it because they know they could be fighting anyone on the card. You're lined up to fight a particular guy but, when the inevitable happens and people start pulling out, your opponent might change in the days or weeks leading up to the fight; even on the day itself. Personally, I don't give a damn who I'm fighting so long as it's a good match-up. I never like to fight anyone who's not in my league. There's just no fun in battering a no-hoper in a matter of seconds – that would make me a bully.

My mood improved instantly when I saw my man inside the club. He was talking to his mates in a corner of the bar and looked up for it.

I had a good look around the place. It was as shady as hell and, as I'd feared, the floor was as hard as concrete. The atmosphere was pretty heavy too and there was that undercurrent of danger that's always kicking around just before a knuckle. The tension can be stifling and there are some really heavy guys on the scene who don't mess around. You've just got to watch what you say and get on with the job in hand.

We knew that some of the gipsies may have been carrying guns that day - this comes with the territory sometimes. I've been in several fights where there have been guys with loaded weapons in the crowd. There have also been occasions – though not at any of my fights and certainly none that has been arranged by Andy – where bullets have been fired.

Guns or no guns, I just love all the pre-match tension before fists-up. While everyone else is on pins, I can't wait to get the show on. Nerves don't bother me: as long as my man turns up and the fight is on, I'm the Ice Man. There had been six fights scheduled for that day and mine was the third. As it happened, there were only three in the end because - surprise, surprise - some of the fighters didn't show.

I said to Andy: "Why can't we get it on now?"

"Okay," he said, but I don't think he realised I meant it because, as I whipped off my jumper and prepared for battle, he looked at me gone out.

"Whoa!" he said. "Have a minute; wait a sec."

But the adrenaline was kicking in now; my blood was up. I just wanted to get on with it, do the business and get home for Coronation Street. I'm a big soap fan: Coronation Street and Emmerdale are my favourites. The fight was scheduled for 2pm. I don't like to fight at night. I prefer it during the day so I can get it over with and get back to the missus and my mates. Besides, I don't normally go out of the village on a Saturday night.

There was some side-betting going on as usual: big, fat wads of notes being pulled out of pockets and thrown down on the wagers table. One of Draper's guys said to me that their man had been knocking people out for fun in their neck of the woods. The Clobberer pointed to me and said: "He'll not be knocking this guy out."

A guy called Dale Hyde, from Wakefield, was in the fight before mine. He asked me if I'd video his fight. I said "no way, mate". I think I'd be physically sick watching two guys going at it.

Before the Hyde fight, Andy had asked me if I'd ref it.

"No way mate," I said. "I couldn't even watch it."

When Hyde and his guy started battling, I turned around and looked the other way. If you watch video footage of the fight on the internet, you'll see all these sturdy guys stood watching the fight, getting all excited and bawling their heads off, and there's me, leaning against a pillar with my back turned, not remotely interested in proceedings, looking towards the bar and occasionally checking my texts. I may not have been watching the fight but I heard enough to tell me that one of these guys was taking a terrible beating. I could hear the crack of fist against skull: a horrible sound.

The fight only lasted a minute-and-a-half at the most; it must have been a total mismatch. I heard this kid go down with a thud. I turned round briefly and saw him laid out on the floor, then turned my head to face the bar again. The lad must have had some balls because he got back up, but then there was another almighty crack and it was all over. I turned round to see Hyde hugging the defeated man and giving him a pat on the shoulder. Now it was my turn.

I whipped my jumper off again and primed myself. I could see Draper dancing around in his corner with a smile on his face. His corner men were geeing him up, telling him to go do the business and reminding him how he'd been knocking out all-comers. They were a rum, feisty lot and seemed convinced their man was onto a winner. There were some big lads among their crowd and they were getting really frenzied now. They were winding their man up big time.

As the noise from their corner became a deafening racket, The Clobberer sidled up to me and whispered: "Put your jumper back on; you'll get cold."

I did as I was told and began my warm-up: one stretch of the arms up, one down. I was ready, but still they delayed, so I took myself off to the toilets and had a little chat with my late nephew Gareth, who I knew would be watching me. I looked up to the ceiling and said: "Let this happen for me and I'll retire."

I nodded to myself, turned around and walked out of the door, straight onto the bar-room floor, where Draper, cocksure and primed, was waiting for me. The ref drew us into the middle. Everybody started closing in around us as Draper put the stare on me. I couldn't be bothered with all that malarkey so I just peered down at my toes like, a bit like a man looking for a stray tenner he's just dropped on the floor. We tapped fists and the roar went up: "Come on, Danny boy!"

Right from the opening shots I knew the guy had talent. I went in at him hard and caught him with some peaches. They were rasping shots to the head but he took them well. The lad was strong, fast and fearless - nailing him wasn't gonna be easy. He had that classic gipsy style of holding out his lead hand like a fishing pole, wiggling it around in front of my face, jabbing at the air in front of him. The supposed aim of this is to keep your man at arm's length while you're trying to find a way through his defences. But that doesn't work with me – I just bide my time and wait for an opening. It wasn't long before I broke through again and that's when I started to hurt him. I ripped a few snorters into his bread basket first. He winced but tucked his chin in well and kept his head down. Then I sent in some huge hooks, smashing them straight into his forehead. He was shook for a moment but regained his balance, so I peppered him with a flurry of jabs, followed by a roundhouse smack in the face. I was hitting him so hard I broke my hand.

The gipsies lay big money on these fights and were getting all worked up as I began to get on top of their man.

"Jab him Danny!" they cried. "Give it to him!"

I battered Draper with a massive left hook/right hook combination that wobbled him. The second one slapped on his face like a whiplash. Then I sent in a big right upper-cut, followed by a venomous right hook, a massive left hand and then a right which landed right on his chin – that one made a right old crack. But still the boy wouldn't go down.

I had a hunch that if I caught him a bit lower, on the bridge of the nose, it would all be over, but he had his head well-protected, so I decided to go even lower. I went for the rib cage first to see if I could break his bones, but I was firing too low, striking him in the liver. Then I tried sending in some bombs to both sides of the ribs, but he moved fast and kept out of the way. I went back to the head but he kept his arms up and elbows out. Anyone in the fist game will tell you that if you go in with a big hook straight into an elbow, your knuckles will shatter - it'd be like punching a brick wall. So, instead of charging back in, I decided to play the waiting game: throw him the bait and reel him in. By now the gipsies had cranked up the decibel level, demanding their man finish the job. They were so loud I couldn't hear my own mates shouting for me. I needed to shut these buggers up so I decided to change tack - and play the old soldier.

Draper came at me like a randy bull - just what I wanted. He threw two big shots that missed - I wasn't happy with that. I didn't mind taking a few belters off him so long as he kept coming forward, but he wasn't getting close enough for me to get in tight and start throwing the big hooks as I like to do. Fortunately, he kept coming at me, taking the bait. I peeled back towards one of the supporting columns in the middle of the bar and he followed me - he must have thought I was flagging. He took a step closer...closer...another step...then...CRUNCH!

First I sent in two big shots to the body followed by a thunderous right hand to the side of his rib cage. Then came a big left to the other side of his ribs which made him wince. Draper was reeling now: I was merciless in my counter-attack. Then: BANG!

I tagged him with what I call a half-and-half shot, a bit like a hook but with a straight arm as you turn the fist. It caught him right on the temple - he went down like a stunned rhino. The boy was badly shaken but got back up. He was a brave man but it didn't take long to put him on his arse again. The knock-out blow was a left-hook cross that floored him. Game over.

Draper's face was a terrible mess and he was bleeding from the mouth. His eyes were so puffed up they were almost completely closed. One of my mates said afterwards that they were the size of the bottom of a pint pot. To be fair, the lad had taken some punishment that day. On the way back home, Psycho said to me: "Jesus, did you see his face? It was proper smashed up. He looked like the Elephant Man!"

Don't get me wrong, Draper had given me some good fist that day, but I didn't half lay into him. If anything, I was holding back a little because I couldn't get rid of that nagging question at the back of my mind: "What if he bangs his head when he goes down?"

My advice to anyone organising a knuckle fight is stay off the concrete and keep to the grass - it might save them a trip to hospital or a spell behind bars.

17) Dawg!

We were like demented ferrets on speed on the way home from the Draper fight. When you have a cast of characters like ours crammed into a Range Rover, it's bound to be colourful.

The Clobberer was at the wheel and there was me in the front, with The Bull, Screaming Skull, Psycho, Nasty Neil, Ashley The Vice and The Undertaker piled into the back: eight Hemsworth lads pumped full of adrenaline, hurtling up the M1 for a post-fight celebration party. My mates might sound like a bunch of villains from a Batman movie, but, I kid you not, you couldn't wish to meet a friendlier bunch of guys. The Undertaker is not the dark, underworld figure you might imagine him to be: I gave him that tag because he's 'buried' a lot of things for me, shall we say.

My mates say the buzz they get from watching me fight is like a drug. I told The Clobberer about the buzz I got from the Draper fight and he said it was just as good on the outside. He's a hard beast, The Clobberer, but even he says that watching me fight is something else. He can't get his head around how I'm laughing and joking before the fight, then, when the time comes and I'm whipping my shirt off, I get the stare on and go to town. Then, when it's all over, I'm shaking hands with the guy and giving him a hug. I put my shirt back on: it's time to get back for the soaps. That's just the way it is with me. One minute the fight's not even on my conscience; I might be thinking about who's just been killed in Emmerdale. Then it's fists-up and The Beast comes out to play!

Sometimes I might say a few words to myself just before I put my gum shield in, but nothing much and not right loud. If I need to pep myself up, I only need to utter two words: "You dawg!"

I don't know where it comes from, but it lurks down there somewhere and comes out in a drawl, a nasty undertone. The 'dog' is whoever needs teaching a lesson at any given time. It might be someone who cuts me up when I'm driving the Beastmobile, or someone being an arse-hole in the pub. It comes out in a hiss: "YOU DAWG!"

I was definitely in a 'dawg' mood before the Draper fight. I think it's because I had upset my family by taking the fight on. My youngest daughter Becky couldn't sleep the night before. When I set off to Leicester, she said to me: "Please come back safe dad; promise me you'll come back safe."

The missus was having kittens too. On the way down to the fight I got a text from her saying: "I love you Dave, but I disagree with what you do."

I sent one back saying: "I'm sorry for what I do."

When I arrived back at the village, we headed straight for the local as usual. As soon as we walked in, everybody stood up, clapping. I couldn't believe they'd all been thinking about me. I'd only told a few people about the fight but so many knew. I looked around the bar and there was Angie with Carla and Becky. They were all there for me - my tablets.

I remember getting the urge to shout, "Hemsworth born and bred!", but I chose not to. I want the town to be proud of me, but, more importantly, I want my dad to be proud of me. Before the fight, my sister had told him that I had something lined up. Dad hates me fighting. He said to her: "He must love getting his face bashed in. Tell him to ring me."

But I didn't – I knew it would only make things worse. I avoided him for weeks but, one morning, we bumped into each other on the forecourt of a petrol station. I was filling up the tank when suddenly his face appeared above the pump next to mine. I knew he was dying to ask me about the fight, but he didn't say a word about it. We were making small talk; I think we were nattering about my sister, who's a singer. It was like a game of cat-and-mouse and the more dad squirmed the more hilarious I found it. He was desperately trying to find a way of raising the subject, but I kept throwing him off the scent. I finally got in my car, chuckling to myself, and he got in his. Game, set and match Beast.

It's funny, you know, to think how my dad hates me fighting so much, but when I win, he's the proudest of the lot. Or maybe it's just relief when I get home in one piece. Angie is the hardest one to deal with before a fight - she absolutely hates the game. I try my hardest not to tell her beforehand, but she always find out. They do get worried, the women. You're treading on eggshells before the day arrives. Angie can read me like a book: women are the masters at mind-reading. Blokes have no hope when it comes to mind games: that's female territory.

Angie's one of those women who can see straight through people. She has no truck with shysters and charlatans; she can spot them a mile off. Our Becky helped get us together. Her friend Jess is Angie's daughter and that's how it started. I was on a bit of a downer after the divorce but life goes on. I'd seen Angie out and about and thought, "chuffing hell, she's nice". My dear old dog Cloud played a part too. I was walking him in the street one day and bumped into Angie. I knew she loved dogs so I told her she could take him for a walk whenever she liked. We got chatting and walked down this path together. We were both pretty nervous. I'm no good with women and conversation; I just don't know what to say. But sometimes things just take their natural course. We ended up at a Crazy Golf place and I plucked up the courage to say: "I don't know how to ask you; I'm not very good with words... I'd like to ask you out on a proper date, but I just don't know how to do it."

Not exactly Casanova stuff!

I said I had a bottle of wine at my place and asked her if she'd like to come round. To my amazement, she said yes!

The next time we met was at her house and things just developed from there. I've been with Angie for 10 years now – we're inseparable. She was my saviour in lean times. The ex-wife basically left me but it was an amicable split as separations go, and I have no hard feelings towards her. There were just problems in the marriage that couldn't be fixed, so I suppose it was for the best that we parted. I've never bad-mouthed her since we divorced and if I saw anybody giving her grief in the pub, I'd step in.

Me and Angie make a great pair: she's the sensible one and I'm the chancer. Her common sense tells her that it's silly for her partner to go on fighting into his 40s. But she's nothing if not flexible and I think deep down she knows I need to fight and that, if I couldn't, I wouldn't be the same man.

That said, when she found out about the Draper fight she threw a right wobbly. She said she was going to leave me at first, then she said she was going abroad. I told her I was going to make this my last one, or at least the second-to-last - I had another one lined up in June, for big money.

As it happened, I got a pittance for the Draper fight. It was about enough for a weekend on the beer and that was about it. No bother - the money is secondary to me. Mind you, Draper did have a side bet on with me: it was like taking candy from a kid!

Up until about eight months before the bout I'd been properly fit and nobody would stand with me on the knuckle scene. At my best I take some beating, even at my age. I know that if I put the work in I'll be right back up there. On the other hand, if I retire there can be no going back. I'd have to stop sparring altogether, move right off the scene.

I know my time in the knuckle game cannot go on forever, but it's so damn hard to turn down a request for a sparring session, let alone a fight. When the call comes in, I just can't help myself. I know what drives me on: it's the knowledge that I was right up there in the glove game, ready to make it seriously big. Then I had that silly accident and my life was turned on its head. Everybody wants to be a name and I'm no different.

I fought Duran when he was past his prime but, for me, the real big time never really happened. I missed my ship, but that's how it is. Fighting in bars and farmers' fields surrounded by cow shit is not what you'd call glamorous, but I'd get the same buzz whether I was battling in a packed arena or a rickety old barn. I'm in heaven when I'm trading blows with a good fighter. After the last punch has been thrown, I'm still buzzing - win or lose. On the way home, the adrenaline makes my muscles twitch. And when I get back to the village and everyone's cheering, I'm off the scale. Then, two or three days later, the dark clouds start drifting in. I get down, start regretting the fight and dissect every little piece of my life. That's the bad part, when the Black Dog starts growling and I begin the long, painful slide back down to earth. When I finally touch down it's with a nasty bump. Boy, it's bad.

This process has been repeating itself for the past 20 years or so: I need the fight, the sparring and the medicine to shake off the blues. But then the very thing that has pulled me out of the doldrums puts me right back in the hole - a big black one with no escape hatch. It's Catch 22 and it's a bummer.

The fight with Draper was different in that I started regretting it as soon as it was over. Perhaps I was thinking about my family, the way I'd try to con the missus, made promises to my kids. I heard someone in the crowd - I think it was one of Draper's guys - say: "This is a man's game!"

"No it's not, it's a foolish man's game," I snapped.

Literally seconds after I'd knocked Draper down for the second time, I was already rueing the fight and getting a bit angry, which is unlike me. It can be a strange mistress, the fight game. You see, deep down, I know it's something I shouldn't be doing. Knowing this gets me down, yet I want to do it again and again and again.

Whether I've been primed up to the max or gone into fights with a paunch, I've never dreaded a fight, no matter who I'm facing. There are no nerves, only the excitement of not knowing what lies ahead. I'm like a child at Christmas who gets everything he asked for.

Yet even someone like me occasionally needs the fires stoking before a battle. It could be something trivial or just an off-the-cuff remark by one of my mates which sets me off. On the way down to the Draper fight, The Clobberer reminded me that it was the anniversary of my nephew's death and that my opponent looked just like a guy who I needed to 'bury'. I'd seen a picture of Draper and he was in fact a dead ringer for this bloke. The Clobberer was winding me up deliberately, saying that Draper didn't know what he was letting himself in for.

"Not only is it the anniversary of your Gareth's death, but your man looks just like the guy you hate," he said with a wink.

I thought, "Chuff me, you're right - he's spitting image!"

And that's all it takes for The Beast to come out of his lair. I may have all these mixed emotions before a fight, but they just get channelled into my one and only thought: "I must destroy this man."

There's no emotion attached to that particular concern: I just have to do the business, pure and simple. One of my biggest trump cards is that I never show my feelings. I might be happy, I might be down; I might have mixed emotions. But, as the hour approaches, I'm a cold fighting machine with only one thing on my mind - victory at all costs. The difference between me and maybe some of the other fighters is that I never get nasty. I hit hard but, if they stay "stop", I stop, and that's the end of it. On the other hand, if they try to head-butt me or take the piss, my head can go and that's when I become extremely dangerous. It's very rare that this happens but when it does, I'm told it's not a pretty sight. Those who have witnessed The Beast in full roar say it's a terrifying spectacle. It's all in the eyes, apparently. They narrow, they glare, they talk - nasty. It's not quite the Incredible Hulk but, believe me, you wouldn't like me when I'm angry!

Just to re-emphasise, this happens very rarely, which is just as well. There are a few types of situations which can bring it on. It might be somebody giving an old man a hard time; it might be someone fighting dirty. Either way, it usually ends up with me delivering my own brand of justice - for they must be disciplined. When it happens, people always say the same thing: "Bloody hell Dave, your eyes! I couldn't believe your eyes."

And it happens just like that: one minute The Gentleman,

next minute The Beast. Don't get me wrong, I'm no Jekyll and Hyde: I'm ordinarily placid and friendly. But just watch out for those eyes - that's the sign that the other me is about to show itself. It hardly ever happens in a fight - that's pure pleasure - but The Beast is always ready to pounce. He's popped up on numerous occasions down the years and it scares me just thinking about it. He was there when I took three guys out in Hemsworth; he was there again when I 'Josephed' that mouthy big shot in Oxford and Herbert finished off his mate. And he was definitely milling around when I timbered three blokes in Barnsley who were being silly boys and giving me some grief. Dawgs!

Jesus, Mary and Joseph, I swear I don't know where it comes from. I can be out having a good night, laughing and joking, and then some idiot upsets me or my friends. It spoils the night and grieves me greatly. Well, it's like rattling The Beast's cage. When they do that I have no respect for them - and that can be very dangerous.

18) Shake Your Money Maker

I've seen fighters get their faces caved in for just a handful of notes. Others have have had their bones smashed to bits for a pittance.

But, for me, there's more than money at stake in the bare-knuckle game. I fight for pride.

If you ask me, it's the noble art in its purest form - the way it used to be. The crowd is usually very respectful and there's hardly ever any trouble. Think of it like this: you've got about 100 extremely-tough guys crammed into a confined area at the same time. Who's gonna be the first to pull anything? It would take a silly man.

Bare-knuckle guys don't chase the dollar the same way the big glove boxers do. The knuckle boys often put their lives on the line for a pittance. Whatever the purse, I'd do anything to stop my opponent destroying me in front of the knuckle crowd. They know their stuff and they come to watch a proper fight. I'd hate to let them down.

One of my favourite ways to stop a good fighter tunnelling into me is to smash his fists and break all his fingers – anything other than surrender. I see the young ones on the scene nowadays, full of spunk and bravado. Some of them can fight for two hours. That's good in one respect but it's hard to take the kind of hammer you get in a bare-fist fight for more than 10 minutes. It's truly brutal and absolutely knackering work, especially for those of us in our 40s!

I've found the best way to train for a knuckle is to allow yourself to get beaten up in sparring. It may sound silly, but it allows your body to absorb maximum punishment. If it means losing a sparring session, so be it. You just take your medicine because you know it's good for you. If you ask me, many of today's young bucks coming through the ranks don't have the heart for this kind of sparring. They think it's all about flooring the guy so he can't carry on. Obviously you want to put your man down when the fight comes around, but more important for a true fighter is the ability to take a punch and carry on trading blows when you're taking a beating. It's the warrior's pride and that is what has kept me going for the past 25 years. I don't do it for the money and I certainly don't like hurting people. It's just what I was born to do.

The gipsies think they own the knuckle scene. They think they're the best fist merchants in the business; that just because they live in a caravan they're better fighters than those who live in a house. True, the knuckle scene is theirs, by and large, and there are some very good gipsy fighters around, but personal experience has taught me that it doesn't matter which side of the tracks you're from: it all comes down to heart at the end of the day. Don't get me wrong, I've got the utmost respect for the gipsy lads, but I just think they take too much for granted. I mean, for goodness' sake, I've lived in a caravan on and off for years, but it doesn't mean I'm a tougher man because of it.

The gipsy boys bring some big, tough men along with them to the knuckles and it can be pretty intimidating at times. But, then again, I'm always surrounded by my posse, and they must look as scary as hell! When the gipsies see me turning up with The Screaming Skull, Psycho and The Clobberer, they must know we'd be ready if anything kicked off. But seriously, you'd do well to see any trouble at the knuckle shows. There's always that danger, of course, but it's extremely rare. The worst I've heard about was a knuckle match in London where it kicked off good style. There was a really nasty atmosphere right from the off and this fella in the crowd got smacked. He walked off but came back 10 minutes later with a loaded gun. He pumped some bullets at the guy who had timbered him but missed with every one – and ended up shooting his own son in the leg!

But this was some time ago and things have changed. You're much more likely to see it go off at a licensed glove night nowadays. Don't get me wrong, the same usual suspects and shady underworld figures are hovering around the edges of both sports. There are some very big businessmen involved in the knuckle world and - it has to be said - some outright criminals, but that's no different to the glove scene.

Some seriously-shady 'businessmen' have been involved in a few of my fights. If there's big money involved, they're all over it like flies round shit. When these guys get their tentacles around the fight, big reputations are at stake because in the 'real' world they might be household names, benefactors or even charity-givers.

The build-up to the fight is so hush-hush that sometimes you wonder if the fixers themselves have forgotten about it. Nobody mentions the fight or the venue until the last possible moment. A conspiracy of silence takes over – nothing can be left to chance. Dozens of people are in on the 'secret', but on-one breathes a word, not even to their nearest and dearest. Even the fighters don't know where they're gonna be fighting. They're told which town or city, but not the venue until the day before the fight. Everything is geared towards keeping the Boys in Blue off the trail because, if they find out, there might be a good many people in a whole load of shit.

The whole business of arranging a knuckle show is so finely-planned yet there are still way too many mismatches because the ranking and weight systems are not as rigid as in the gloved game. All it takes to get a knuckle on is a few phone calls to the right people. Take my fight with the Leicester Bulldog: one day I was watching a DVD of one of his fights and I said to my mate Butch that I'd take on him or his opponent. That was all it took to start the ball rolling. A few phone calls later and I was lined up to fight The Dog – this all happened in the space of a week. There's no pissing about in the knuckle game; none of the hassle that goes with a gloved match. You agree to your share of the purse and your man agrees to his. Then you decide whose turf you'll be fighting on and Bob's your uncle – you've got a match. Let's worry about the venue later.

I ended up fighting the Dog for just £500. I've earned a lot more from knuckle fights in the past: it just depends whose involved in the set-up. I was once offered £20,000 for one fight but I turned it down. That may seem crazy, but when you've seen what I've seen in this game, and you know what I know, it wasn't such a bad move, believe me. In short, I didn't want my legs blown off if I'd lost. When the Big Rollers lay a lot of money on you, they expect a return. If they don't get it, then watch out.

Side-betting is the norm and there's always the danger that if the Big Rollers lose a massive wad of cash that they've staked on their man, they might come looking for him. Now I'm not afraid to fight anybody, but these guys don't argue with their fists. They play by their own rules and that may include mutilation, death or both.

Not so long back, my old foe Draper rang me with a message from James Quinn McDonagh, the King of the gipsy bare-knuckle world. McDonagh was the star of the show in a recent TV documentary about gipsies and fist-fighting. No-one could beat him.

Draper asked me if I'd fight with McDonagh and nine other bare-knucklers in the United States. Apparently, James wanted to form a kind of 'dream team' comprising some of the best knucklers in the UK. I was naturally flattered to be asked but, as much as I liked and respected James, I had to say no. There was no way I was going to fight in the States with anyone: my name doesn't carry there. I've made my name here, in my own country. I fight for my family name, just like the gipsies do.

That said, I'd love to be able to fight alongside James one day - in the UK, of course. Maybe somewhere down the line we share blood lines: my great-grandfather was an Irish tinker from Belfast. My grandparents were all from the old country: the McNichols on one side and the Ryans on the other. They were mainly from southern and mid-west Ireland. So we're just a bunch of Micks really, with a bit of tinker thrown in.

19) Holmfirth

I had my first taste of glove work when I started palling around with a lad called Pete Wiggins. I was about 17 at the time and I had just started fighting for Hemsworth YMCA.

Pete would come to the club with me three times a week. He was - and still is - a very faithful friend and a bloody good fighter. We used to do a bit of pad and bag work round at his house in Hemsworth – they were great days.

Me and Pete used to watch Fight Night together on Saturdays, when Duran, Sugar Ray and Hagler were in their prime. Boy, what fighters they were. We used to love watching these guys scrap. Marvin Hagler was our biggest hero – Pete even called his dog Marvin.

Another hero of ours was the British middleweight Tony Sibson: 'Sibbo', we called him. He was a hell of a fighter and won the Commonwealth and European belts. He had a shot at the world title too when he fought Hagler, but lost on a technical knock-out. Hagler practically finished him, but he was great, was Sibbo. His record speaks for itself: 55 wins in 63 bouts – 31 of those victories coming from a knock-out. Good old Sibbo.

I'll never forget watching those big 15-rounders with my old mate Pete. I remember watching Hagler vs Suygar Ray in a fight that was so brutal you thought there was no way it could go the distance. But not only did it go the full 15 rounds, they both came out for the final round like it was the first. These guys had been giving each other the most almighty beating and they finished the fight like they'd started it!

With Hagler, Hearns and co., it was close, intense fighting from the word go, real gladiator stuff. They threw everything bar the kitchen sink at each other for 15 rounds. I remember they would hardly ever break off each other – it was as if they were fighting in a phone box, just the way I like to. These guys were my heroes not only because they were great fighters, but because you knew they would fight to the death if they had to.

I would never pretend to be in the same class as Hagler, Sugar Ray or Duran, but what I do share with them is a fighter's heart. I would rather die than give in to a better man. I wouldn't say I've got a chin like granite, but I'm a stubborn old sod – I refuse to go down. I will never accept I'm too hurt to carry on. Seriously, you'd have to chop my arms and legs off before I gave in. Not even broken bones will stop me – just ask Danny Ryan. I fought the Irishman in Belfast in what turned out to be a really tough scrap. I broke my right fist in the second round. I was in agony but I carried on and went the distance with him. It ended in a draw.

After the fight I bandaged my own hand and put a pot on myself using a special type of cement, then went straight back to work. The pot held firm and did the trick – until I nearly broke my hand again trying to get it off!

I like to heal my own wounds. It's the same with cuts - I stitch them myself. I remember once pulling my skin up to get a stitch in and I could see the edge of my facial bones. Blood was gushing out of the cut, so on that occasion I had to go the hospital where a nurse glued it for me. But I've found that normally you can do the job just as well yourself.

My face has taken the brunt of the damage down the years but it's my hands that will never heal properly. The knuckles are skewed and my bones so brittle that I can't shake people's hands properly anymore. I get shooting pains in my right hand now and again and it hurts like hell. It's quite normal for me to go into a fight with a broken hand or nose. I once went the distance with a guy called Kevin Thompson despite him breaking my snout in the third round. The fight, which was held at The Barbikan in York, was shown live on Sky TV and close-ups showed that my nose had caved in. It was sheer willpower that got me through; I just shut the pain off and kept boxing. I ended up losing by dent of a silly knock-down when I was off-balance.

It's hard to describe the pain of fighting with a broken nose. When people ask me to describe it I tell them to imagine they've got a wobbly tooth and that someone is prodding it 50 times in one round – that gives you some idea of the pain you're in when you're being constantly jabbed on a broken pecker. It's only the adrenaline pumping round your body that makes it even slightly bearable.

But busted bones only hurt when you've lost. If you win, the endorphins and adrenaline kick in and you don't feel a thing. But a few days later you start suffering, particularly if you've got a broken hand or cracked ribs. If that's the case you're in big trouble - the pain lasts for weeks. In a funny way, that first week or two after a tough fight, when you're nursing broken bones and swollen eyes, is a lovely thing despite the immense pain and suffering you're going through. Every little task you normally take for granted becomes a challenge - you can't even stroke your nose when it's sore.

The bit I like the most is crawling off the settee using my elbows (because my hands are too sore to rest on) and slowly making my way towards the kitchen to make myself a cuppa. The satisfaction you get from accomplishing this everyday task is immense. It may sound strange, but it's as if you've done something for the world. Any boxer who has come out of a fight in a bad way will know exactly what I mean by this. But I bet none of them spill their tea down their front when they finally get back to the sofa – that's my speciality!

When the bones finally start to heal and my head begins to clear again, there's only one place I want to be: Holmfirth. I love the place. It's the only place me and Angie really feel that we're away from it all. I feel at ease in this sleepy little West Yorkshire town, which is just north of the Peak District. Me and Angie just can't get enough of it.

Holmfirth is famous for being the location for Last of the Summer Wine, the TV comedy series about three old Tykes who keep getting into mischief. You can actually go and get a bite to eat at Sid's Café and walk up Nora Batty's Steps. But, for us, it's the peacefulness of the place that we adore. There's no pressure there, no lurking dangers, no mither whatsoever. You don't see many young people in the pubs and everyone just minds his own business. We've got a caravan there and go whenever we can. Many people don't believe me when I tell them this, but I love it when it's raining in Holmfirth – and rain it often does – because, when it's pissing down outside, I'm snuggled up under the covers, as warm as toast. It's like being back inside the womb.

Hardly anybody recognises me in Holmfirth but even there the odd person will come up to me and want to shake my hand. Sometimes they'll stare and, being a Hemsworth lad - where it's every man for himself - I'll think they're angling for a scuffle. I remember once, me and the missus were sat in a pub watching this guy at the dartboard. Every time he threw a dart he turned round and stared straight at me. I said to the missus: "Have you seen that bloke over there? You watch what he does when he throws the darts."

She was a bit perplexed, so I said: "Just watch."

And sure enough the bloke kept staring over from the oche. We felt a bit uncomfortable so we moved to the other room, where we got talking to another bloke who said he recognised me from fights he'd seen on Youtube. He said there was another bloke in the pub who was a big fan of mine and I asked who he was. He pointed to the man in the pink top who was playing darts, the same guy who'd been ogling us from the dart board!

I told the guy I thought the darts player had been hankering for a fight. The guy chortled and said: "Chuffing hell, he idolises you!"

20) "Wait there 'til I get me slippers!"

It just goes to show you can never really tell what someone's intentions are just from their demeanour. The thing is, I'm sort of conditioned to respond to threats, or perceived threats at least. It's a fighter's instinct and it's stood me in good stead in the past. The way I see it, you take no chances. It's either fight or flight, and if the other guy doesn't take 'no' for an answer, I fight.

The guy at the dart board turned out to be a friendly type – in fact, we're good friends now - but he could just as easily have wanted trouble. Sometimes the problem is that a lot of fellas look at me and see Dave Radford the hard man, not the real guy underneath. I'm one of the nicest guys you could wish to meet, but, because of the way I look, some people, like the darts player in Holmfirth, are scared to come up to me and say hello. This in itself can cause tension: you don't know what the other guy is thinking or why he's staring at you. Just come over here and let me buy you a drink man.

I've lost count of the number of times I've been threatened or verbally abused when I'm out on the tiles. Most of the time it's in another town or city, which is one of the reasons I don't like to leave the village at the weekend. When I go for a night out in a strange place, people don't know my reputation, and this in itself can lead to trouble. There was one incident in Leeds fairly recently when I went for a night out with The Undertaker, Psycho and some other mates. I had a bad feeling about the night before we'd even set off: I often gets this feeling and I'm usually proved right. Everything was going okay until we came across this drunk in the street who was having a go at his missus. We told him to cool it but he started getting all shirty and threatened to cave my head in.

I said: "Look pal, I don't want any trouble; I just want you to lay off her."

Eventually he got the message that I wasn't the kind of guy to be messed with and started to calm down. Him and his missus were out-of-towners like us and were heading for the railway station, so we followed just behind them to make sure the girl was okay and that he didn't kick off again. As luck would have it, they got on the same train as us and we sat next to them on the ride home. By this stage the guy had cooled and was even being quite courteous, but the way he he'd been speaking to his girlfriend was disgraceful. That's not how a man is supposed to behave towards a woman, not in my book anyway. Before we parted I left him with a few choice words. The next day I got a text from him saying he was sorry and thanking me for stopping him laying into his missus!

There have been other occasions when what might have turned into a very nasty incident ended in hilarity and farce. I'm thinking in particular of the day a gang of rough-house Geordies came to play in our neck of the woods. The atmosphere was poisonous.

We were in a pub in Hemsworth called Whispers and there were swarms of local lads milling around, looking none too pleased with these big-mouth Geordie guys, who were necking ale for fun. I was about 25 at the time and the Geordies were all in their early 30s. They went outside to get in a minibus and got into some trouble with some local lads. Somebody came into the pub and said: "Dave, you better get out there. There's gonna be trouble."

I walked outside and saw a ring of Hemsworth lads surrounding this one Geordie. He must have been a crazy kid because, like one of those Indian braves making a last stand surrounded by Apaches, he was pointing at the Hemsworth lads and shouting: "Come on, any one of you now! I'll fight any one of you."

It was about to kick off, then someone said, "Dave Radford's here", and everyone looked round towards me, their heads moving at exactly the same time.

For some reason that is still unknown to me, I bellowed: "I'm Spartacus!"

Everyone shut up instantly and started to giggle. All eyes were now on the Geordie guy to see how he'd react, but he just looked at me as if to say: "No thanks – you look like you can fight."

The situation had been defused and the Geordie boy got his arse out of there double-quick. He put his hand up in a sort of 'white flag' gesture and hopped on the bus. A big cheer went up for Spartacus!

If ever I'm confronted with trouble anywhere near the house, I make sure I get my slippers on first. I like to fight in my slippers because they're nice and comfy, and it means I don't get my shoes scuffed. They're the kind of slippers you'd see your granddad wearing, those with the snuggly fluff inside. Sometimes I'd go on nights out with my slippers on - and fight in them if necessary – because I'd forgotten to take them off.

Whenever I have to go outside the house to deal with a situation, I wind masking or gaffer tape around my slippers so they don't fall off while I'm scuffling. Sometimes, when I'm out but near enough to home, and some hoodlum wants a fight, I'll nip back to my gaff and get my slippers on.

One time a guy came round our house and rapped on the door, wanting to have it out with me. I said: "Wait there 'til I get my slippers on!"

I rushed up to my bedroom, wound the gaffer tape around my fighting vessels so they looked enough like steel toe-caps for my liking, and then belted it back downstairs. When I reached the front door the guy took one look at my nifty footwear, then looked up into the Face of The Beast, and scarpered. His face was a picture.

Most people's slippers last three years tops, but mine last practically a lifetime - that's because mine are fortified! I've used them for all sorts of occasions, even gone running in them. I love my slippers. If you wind that gaffer tape around them tightly enough, they're good as a shoe, no word of a lie. I used to walk in the King's Head wearing my best shirt and slippers, having forgotten to take them off. There'd be a few sniggers, of course, but it didn't bother me one bit.

"What's the crack?" I'd say.

"What the fuck have you come out in your slippers for?"

"Cos they're comfy."

Truth is, I'm so used to wearing them that sometimes I don't even know I've got them on. They're so comfortable I just forget. I've even been round Wakefield with them on.

There have been other times when it would have been wiser not to have rushed out of the house to deal with the situation in hand, slippers or no. I'm thinking in particular of the night we spotted a trespasser in our back garden who seemed very interested in knowing what was inside our shed. I'd just come out of the bath and had a towel round my waist, but I was so keen to catch the little blighter I ran straight out of the house with the towel still around me. I charged out like Tarzan, but as soon as I burst through the back door the burglar jumped over our garden fence and legged it down the street. I charged after him and somehow the towel stayed wrapped around my waist. The little scallywag ran down a neighbour's drive and into their back garden. I dashed straight down the driveway and onto the lawn, where I saw him hopping over a fence. I ran after him, put one leg on the fence to pull myself up, but the towel unfurled and dropped to the ground, leaving my bare knackers dangling in the wind. I looked down at my balls in horror and was about to pick up the towel when I saw a pair of faces staring down at me from an upstairs window in my neighbour's house. They seemed unbelievably calm in the circumstances.

Meanwhile, panic froze me to the spot. I knew that any second now I'd have to bend over and pick the towel up. I had a dilemma: do I walk slowly backwards so as not to expose my arse (bearing in mind they'd already seen my balls) or do I turn around and pick the towel up, exposing my neighbours to the dark side of the moon? It was a big decision in the circumstances and it all happened so quickly I've forgotten which option I chose. All I remember is grabbing the towel and quickly wrapping it round my waist, before hopping it back to our house as fast as my bare feet would carry me. Meanwhile, the burglar had disappeared into the night, scuttled off back to his little rat-hole. It's a pity for him, really, because if I'd have caught him, he'd have had the privilege of being the first man to see Dave Radford give someone a hiding with his tackle out.

There's nothing worse than someone violating the safety of your family home. My kids were still living with us at the time, which is why I risked baring my arse in the neighbourhood to catch the little rodent. My daughters are everything to me and I see it as my duty in life to keep them safe from the horrors of this world. Carla and Becky are in their early 20s now but I still tell them - as I do Angie - that every time they go to bed and turn their lights off, all the lights in the world go out as far as I'm concerned. Me and our Carla are like two peas in a pod. We were born on the same day, May 30, and when she was brought into this world, on my 19th birthday, she weighed 7lb 11oz, when her old man's fighting weight was 11st 7lb. Strange that.

My daughters love dogs so one day I bought them a pooch called Cloud, a Weirmaraner. The missus and the kids loved him, but I always pretended not to give two hoots about the mutt. We got him because the kids were always pestering me to get a dog. I didn't want one, but of course it was me who ended up looking after the bugger. Hence the name Cloud – the big black cloud that would hover over me for ever and a day. Of course, as time passed I came to love the mutt. When everybody was home I would pretend to ignore him, not wanting them to think I was a soft touch with animals. But when they'd all gone out and it was just me and Cloud, I'd love that mutt to pieces, give him loads of kisses and cuddles. I don't know why I was so afraid to show my softer side around Cloud – maybe I was trying too hard to play Dad. If truth be told, I absolutely adored that pesky pooch. We were all heartbroken when he died.

When Cloud was alive I used to have a recurring dream about Roberto Duran coming round to our house and our beloved pet doing his business on the kitchen floor right in front of him. I used to wake up in cold sweats thinking it was real. I never smacked him though, not even in my dreams.

So yes, I am a big softy at heart and I'm over-protective with my kids. Maybe it's because of the losses and the heartache I've endured in the past. My kids used to laugh at me for the things I would do to keep them out of harm's way. When Becky got a new pair of roller boots in her teens, for instance, it drove me crazy with worry. Her mates all had roller-blades but we got Becky those old-fashioned ones with stoppers on the front because I thought they were safer. When she went out roller-blading with her mates I imagined all kinds of horrors that might come her way. I was absolutely convinced she would she would fall and hurt herself; maybe graze her knees, hit her head on the concrete or even break a leg. I'd be pacing the floor until she came home. I would drive myself potty with worry, so I decided that something had to be done. The next time she went out with her roller boots on I got some small cushions from the settee and gaffer-taped them to her elbows and knees. Her mates might have laughed, but at least I knew she'd be safe from harm. I'm a make-do-and-mend sort of guy, so this seemed the logical thing to do, but my daughters were in hysterics.

Gaffer-taped slippers and cushion knee pads are two of my quirkier inventions, but there have been a whole lot more. My creations have never really caught on in the wider world, which I think is a shame really.

21) Rumble in the Park

At the arse end of possibly the worst summer on record, I fought the 'Dark Destroyer' Nigel Benn in my home town.

It was a bitterly-cold day in that weird summer/autumn period when the supposedly sunnier days start retreating and winter starts knocking on the door. Local boxing promoter Andy Booker had organised it as a charity event. It was to be held at Hemsworth Miners' Welfare's football ground, and me and Benn were the big draw. We'd agreed to fight each other in a three-round exhibition, which was to be preceded by several under-card fights involving fighters from Yorkshire and Lancashire.

'Rumble in the Park', as it was called, was set for September 17, 2012, and word was that the whole town would be turning out for what I was intending to make my retirement fight. In the weeks leading up to the 'Rumble', the rumours were that Benn was going to come out fighting, exhibition or not. That was fine with me - if he tried any real rough stuff then the White Destroyer would give back as good as he got.

I'd heard that Benn had fought in some exhibition bouts all over the UK and was in tip-top condition for his age. He was 48, five years older than me, but he'd put all the bad shit behind him: a lot of silly stuff, things he got into after he retired that he shouldn't have. Apparently he'd found God and all was well with the man again.

The Clobberer was on the Rumble card too - it was going to be a great day for the town, which doesn't have a great deal to shout about nowadays, what with the pits having closed down and unemployment sky-high. This would be our chance to give them something to smile about, put on a proper show for the townsfolk. When Craig heard who was on the card he was nearly crying with joy. He said to me: "I can't believe I'm gonna be fighting on the same card as my hero."

"You mean Benn?" I said.

He laughed, shook his head, and said: "No – Dave Radford!"

As is my custom nowadays, I barely trained for the fight. I think the only thing I did by way of preparation was to try to keep my weight down a bit. My daughter told me that baby sweet potatoes were good for you and stopped you piling on the pounds, so I gorged on them for weeks! I'm lucky in that I have a natural fitness which allows me to get through my bare-fist and exhibition fights with little or no preparation. As expected, a huge crowd turned out for the Rumble. There were about 2,000 people there but it seemed like the whole town had come out. As usual, I was completely relaxed in the hours leading up to the fight and, just before setting off, I had my feet up watching Coro - I wouldn't miss it for the world.

When I arrived at the football ground, I could see that Team Benn had arrived in a fleet of 4X4s. I walked through the turnstiles and made my way past hordes of people patting me on the back and wishing me luck. It must have taken me a good 15 minutes to get from the turnstiles to the changing rooms, where I finally saw Benn surrounded by his acolytes, going through his moves with his hoodie on. He looked in prime physical condition. When he saw me enter the room he came straight over with a big, friendly smile and offered me his hand. It was a nice gesture and he seemed like a really nice bloke. We had a little chat and agreed that we would both take the sting out of our shots and make it a proper exhibition. There would be no knock-outs, nothing too heavy. We left it at that and Benn went off to the marquee to do a photo shoot and have his picture taken with the paying guests. Fair play to Nigel, he was a good sport that day and made time for everyone. He put a smile on his face, signed photos for the kids and was an all-round good egg. You can't say that about too many big-time fighters - charity do or not.

The ring was on the edge of the football field and surrounded by VIP tables where those who'd paid top whack got a catering service. MC Charlie Hale was warming the crowd up with a comedy routine that could best be described as unique. He introduced the first two fighters - a guy from Barnsley and a Blackpool kid. But everyone's attention was focused on the raven-haired glamour puss in the Barnsley guy's corner. Where on earth had she come from? I'd never seen her on the scene before and I'd certainly never seen a female corner woman at any of my fights. She was wearing designer shades which she didn't take off all afternoon – and it wasn't even sunny. Right from the word go she was shouting and bawling at her charge as he took a battering from The Blackpool Rock. And what a battering it was. The Lancashire lad had the better of it and severely hurt his man, but the other lad was a plucky fighter too and gave the other guy a cut above the eye. It was the Lancashire guy who got the nod from the ref after three rounds of intense battling. Good fighter that lad.

Next up was The Clobberer. Well he gave his man some right fist. I was watching from the crowd and really felt for the lad he was battling because I know what it's like to be on the end of Craig's hammer blows, and that day on the soccer ground he was really in the mood. I winced when he sent in The Claw shots. His opponent, a Doncaster lad, looked shell-shocked and a tad scared. His chest and arms were covered in red marks where Craig had been peppering him with huge body shots. Craig's no spring chicken himself. He was 41 at the time and his opponent in his early twenties. But even though Clobberer was visibly tiring as early as the second, he gave the lad a right pasting. I felt sorry for the kid – not only was he up against the dreaded Claw, but he had the screaming banshee barking at him through cosmetic lips. And all the while Craig was following this kid around the ring with those killer eyes. The lad kept trying to back off but The Clobberer kept cornering him at the ropes, where he gave him an awful bashing. Jesus, Mary and Joseph! He was whanging some proper screamers into the poor guy's ribs as the she-devil kept on barking into his lugs. There's no way I could have a screaming harridan like that in my corner; it'd drive me crackers. The ring is no place for a woman in my book.

The Clobberer walked his bout and now it was time for the 'Clash of the Titans'. The Dolly Mixtures, a local girl band, had just finished off their set when I walked out to the tune of an old Irish folk song called The Foggy Dew, by the Dawn Green Stompers. I'm a big fan of Irish folk music, if you haven't already guessed.

I marched up to the ring wearing a white silk robe and white shorts with 'The Dog' stitched onto one side in black letters. As expected, I got a thunderous reception which gave me that old pre-bout tingle down my spine. Then Benn glided into the ring, calm and cocksure, looking mean like the Benn of old. He looked bigger than I'd expected and very fit. The MC introduced him as "the best British fighter of all time" and me as a "local hero" who had never been put down in over 120 fights outside the ring. Just for the record, I've had a few glove fights as well!

Me and Nigel gave each other a hug and then got stuck in. We both stuck to the script, but when you're fighting a natural-born scrapper like Benn, a man of the streets, there are times when his natural aggression is gonna come roaring out. I remember, after one of the famous Benn/Eubank matches in the 90s, Eubank - who won that particular battle - said the man he had just been fighting couldn't have been human. He said that Benn was an animal - not as an insult, but as a mark of respect.

Well, let me tell you, even at 48 that animal still had some bite left. In the third he caught me with some bombs that reminded me just why he'd held world-title belts in two different divisions. Like all world-class boxers who are getting on a bit, he may have lost some of his speed and agility, but he's lost none of his punching power. Halfway through the third he banged me with a right which made me dizzy. It really shook me and I was thinking of letting the big right go, but I chose not to. I thought if it did turn nasty I'd either have to pull away - which is never an option for me - or try to discipline him. What I had to keep in mind was that this man still had it in him to make a good fighter look like a pussy, and I didn't want that in front of my home fans.

There were times when he was toying with me and others where I knew I'd caught him with a good 'un. Towards the end it did turn a bit farcical, with Benn clowning around and playing up to the crowd with his Eubank impersonations. I have to admit that I started it when I pretended to kick him up the arse after the first round.

22) Watch out for the Eyes!

A few weeks after the Benn fight I was on the card to fight at 'A Night with Mike Tyson' at the Barnsley Metrodome, but right up until the last minute I was in two minds whether to go or not. I had a wedding and a funeral to go to that day – talk about a mix of emotions.

I saw Angie's niece get married and a friend put to rest, then I jumped in a car and went to fight this Scouse bloke who was supposed to be very handy, but whose name I still don't remember. Everyone on the local boxing circuit had been looking forward to the show. Tyson would be entertaining the crowd with stories about his chequered life and career. Before the event there was a local campaign, led by women's-rights activists, to get the show called off. The campaigners bent the ear of local-newspaper editors and politicians about how disgraceful it was that a convicted rapist should be allowed to appear as a hero figure at a local venue. Despite the furore, the show went ahead. I was to be one of the minions providing the blood and sweat between Tyson's anecdotes and his joshing with the crowd. Andy Booker, who's a big mate of Tyson's, organised the show, and, as usual, he wanted me involved.

Andy got to know Tyson in the most unusual of circumstances – the accounts of how they became friends differ depending on who you are speaking to – but I know that Iron Mike is quite a regular visitor to Andy's home in Doncaster. Apparently he loves Andy's Sunday roasts.

Tyson was the star attraction for the show in Barnsley and, despite the women's-rights activists getting all uppity about the whole thing, every one of the 1,000 seats was taken. The atmosphere on the night was great and Mike was in one of his better moods. After beating the Scouser I was in high spirits too, but when I came out of the changing rooms my mood soured instantly. I saw these security men getting all shirty with people who'd paid good money to watch the show. All they were doing was trying to get their pictures taken with Tyson but these arse-hole security guys were trying to stop them. Maybe it was because I was pissed off at not being able to land a good left hook on the Scouse guy, but these Neanderthals in security jackets really wound me up. Needless to say, The Beast, who had been in hibernation for quite some time, made an appearance. I knew he was on the loose because my eyes had blanked over. I strode over to where some of my people were. I wanted to find out what the hell was going, but then this bouncer grabbed hold of my arm and tried to pull me back. Dawg!

He was being all clever, asking me what the fuck I thought I was doing. I tried to ignore him, told him I was looking for Andy, but he kept on being a smart-arse with me. I turned round to face him and growled: "You ever speak to me like that again and I'll put you straight on your fucking arse!"

The eyes had almost gone. I pointed to my hands and said: "These'll do my talking in a minute!"

Meanwhile, my friend The Clobberer was taking photos to wind the bouncers up and everything was getting a bit out of control. Thankfully, one of my mates came over and calmed me down, otherwise it could have got really nasty. When The Gentleman packs his bags and The Beast comes out to play, anything can happen. The moron bouncer sensed this and suddenly changed his tune. Maybe he saw the way I was eyeing his chin: I was dying to smash a left hook into it. Honestly, these fellas put a suit on and think they're the bee's knees. They had spoiled what had been a fantastic night's entertainment and it grieved me so much I just wanted to get the hell out of there. I didn't even stick around for my 'testimonial'. The organisers had wanted Iron Mike to deliver a fitting tribute to The Beast on his impending retirement and present me with a little something. Sod that – I was out of there quicker than you could say "I'm out of there".

The word was that Tyson was gonna present me with a little something to bring the curtain down on my career, but I didn't give him the chance even if this was the case. I'd been to a mate's funeral and my niece's wedding that day, then fought a tough Scouser and had a run-in with some monkeys in suits. I was in no mood for testimonials.

In the changing rooms after the fight, people had been streaming in to offer me handshakes. Some asked me to come over to their table to meet their wives and kids. These were people I hadn't seen in years. It's like this on the boxing circuit: people come and go all the time and they reappear when you least expect it. There were a few lads there who I hadn't seen since my early twenties, such as my old mate Chris, who brought back some fond memories. He told me he'd been working in a foreign country back in the 90s and while he was having a glass of lager in a bar after work, he saw me going at it with Roberto Duran on TV. He said he was that gobsmacked he almost spat his beer out.

When I told him I'd been plastering my sister's bedroom wall just before the fight he nearly fell off his chair laughing. It was no laughing matter fighting the bastard, Chris.

23) The Invisible Man

A week before the fight in Barnsley I was in the pub, pissed up, when Booker rang, asking if I would fight. I hadn't been in the gym for three months and I was in no shape to take on the Scouse kid, but, me being me, I said yes. The scorpion wins again!

On the morning of the show, I was at the George & Dragon for the funeral reception of a mate who'd died on a plane on his way to a holiday in Spain. I was drinking cups of tea but my mates were telling me to forget the fight and get pissed. I was tempted, but I had every intention of making this my last gloved bout so I stuck to the char, thinking I might as well get the last one over with before I hung up the gloves. I spent the rest of the afternoon at Angie's niece's wedding – a bereavement and a marriage on the same day!

While everyone was getting pissed and having a good time, I was sipping Yorkshire tea, thinking that I could well do without this shite (the fight, not the wedding). I didn't even know the name of the guy I was supposed to be fighting. As it happened, he turned out to be a proper tough nut but I was all over him from the start. The ref stopped it with about 10 seconds to go in the final round. The guy was wincing in the corner; it seemed to me like he was crying. The ref jumped in and I stepped back. It's just as well really because I was cream-crackered. Midway through the final round I screamed at the timekeeper: "How long's left?!"

There was nothing left in the tank again - I was knackered from the first bell. To tell the truth, I was knackered going up the steps to get in the ring! That morning, before the wedding, the funeral and the fight (sounds like a Hugh Grant movie!), I went upstairs to get changed and, by the time I got back down to the bottom of the stairs, I was huffing and puffing like an old sea lion. I sat down on the bottom step and there was the missus, watching me with a look of utter disdain.

"What's the matter with you?" she said. "I thought you

were supposed to be fighting tonight!"

Suffering Jesus, I've fought in some states before but that takes the biscuit. On top of everything else, I was full of cold, I'd pulled my back at work and I was getting shooting pains in my right hand. When I woke up on the morning of the fight my back had seized up completely, so I necked some tablets before setting off for Barnsley.

I will say this about that Liverpudlian – he was a crafty bleeder. I've come up against his sort many times over the past 20-odd years. They're so infuriating because they turn on their side and make themselves 'invisible': it's like trying to punch a washing line.

This guy had me in a rage because I couldn't land the Big Left on his chin or in the solar plexus. It's always the same with these types: they land nothing for ages and then, BOOM! They tag you with a good 'un.

One haymaker from the Scouser struck me so hard it felt like it had come from the other side of Barnsley. I had him in my pocket for the whole fight but he was too quick to be caught with the Big One. Fighters like him are so hard to put down. It's like fighting the Invisible Man.

There are lots of clever lads like him around – they're slippery eels and it's hard to lay a glove on them. The Scouser knew I was trying to set up the big left hook but he kept manoeuvring out of the way so I couldn't land it. Even though I ended up winning, I was peeved that I hadn't given the crowd full value for all the money they'd coughed up. I hate to see people being short-changed and it makes me furious when little jobsworths piss people about to make themselves feel important. When I saw those security wallahs stopping people having their picture taken with Tyson, just because they hadn't paid top whack, it made my blood boil. I could feel my eyes beginning to change, which is not a good sign.

But I went through all the motions, had my photo taken with Tyson and shook his hand. We had a little chat and I told him he looked well. He was in good spirits that night. I'd met him three or four times before and sometimes he can be very moody, not wanting to speak to anyone. So fair play to Mike and Andy, but those security guys can go and screw themselves.

24) Left Back in the Changing Rooms

Bouncers have always been a bit wary of me. They take one look at my face and see trouble.

I've got one of those appearances that will bring fear to some and present a challenge to others. Some people look at me and say: "You've been in a few rugby games haven't you mate!"

I'll josh with them for a while; tell them I play for Hemsworth Miners Welfare. Then they'll ask me what position I play and I can't keep up the bullshit any longer.

"Left back in the dressing room," is my usual response.

I really haven't got a clue about rugby or any other sports – all I know is the ring. I've never been a player of anything really: I'm a fighter through and through. I don't really watch any sports but, sometimes, on a Sunday morning, I'll watch Rugby League on TV. Now that's a real man's sport. I find it fascinating to watch these huge, strapping fellas come out of a scrum and get a bollocking from these tiny referees. You see the ref giving them a right old ear-bashing, wagging his finger at them and shaking his head, and these giant fellas just bow their heads like naughty schoolboys and take it. They've clearly got a lot of respect for the referee, which is more than can be said for those prima-donna footballers. I think these pampered pricks should be made to play rugby once a month to learn what a real man's game is about. The way they dive and try to con the ref is an absolute joke. It grieves me when they roll on the ground like they do – that Ronaldo fella particularly irks me. What do these people tell their wives after a match when they know they've cheated? I wouldn't be able to look my missus in the eye. To go down when you haven't been touched is unthinkable to the likes of me and The Clobberer: you'd have to blow our legs off first. We train our bodies to stay upright no matter what.

But not all 'boxers' are like us and that's why I choose my sparring partners carefully. The saying goes that no man is a coward who steps in the ring, yet there are some who shouldn't be in there in the first place. They call themselves boxers but they don't have the heart to be a fighter in the true sense. You don't become a fighter just by sticking on a pair of gloves and winning a few amateur fights. To really test your mettle, you've got to take a few beatings and still come out smiling. But there are some guys who just don't have it in them. There was a time, a few years ago, when barely anyone was prepared to challenge me on the bare-knuckle scene. They'd heard about my reputation and preferred to lose out on their purse rather than step on the cobbles with me. Mr Platts once backed me for a bare knuckle by offering a highly-fancied guy - who shall remain anonymous - a grand to fight me, but such was my reputation that he turned down the offer. He stood to make a thousand notes just by taking me on, but feared me so much he bottled out of it. Suffering Jesus, I'd have fought for nothing.

I train the youngsters at my gym to be fighters in my own image – warriors but not bullies. Sometimes I'm brought to tears watching them fight and there are times when I just can't look. Don't get me wrong, I have no qualms about pummelling a man into submission inside the ring, but the young ones are a different matter. As long as we can keep them off the streets, out of harm's way, I'm a happy man.

It's great to be able to provide the young ones with somewhere safe and warm where they can learn the disciplines of the art. It's much better than beating the crap out of each other on the street or getting smashed over the head with a beer bottle.

There are some good lads coming through in our neck of the woods and I'd hate to see them throw it all away by going down the wrong path. Scott Askam is a cage fighter cut from the same Hemsworth granite as me. He's only in his mid-20s but he's already made a name for himself in The Cage. He's a nice, respectable young lad and if he keeps putting the work in, he'll be the next star of the town. Scott reminds me a bit of myself when I was his age. I learned to fight at the local YMCA and it kept me off the streets, whereas some of my mates were getting into bother because they had nowt else to do. There were some good old blokes at the YMCA who taught me a lot about respect, hard work and discipline. As I got older I wanted to pass this on to the youngsters in our village, so when I got enough money together, I opened a gym above the King's Head and charged nothing for membership. We had so many members that eventually we had to move to a bigger place above the Alpha Club further down town. My old mate Roberto Duran opened the gym in September 2010. What a great honour it was for the great man to come to our little town and cut the ribbon at my new gaff. He's been over our way quite a few times since our rumble in Africa. In fact I was supposed to fight him again in an exhibition match in Doncaster, but the fight didn't happen for one reason or another. Instead, we ended up giving after-dinner speeches at Skellow Club.

I'm always gong to some black-tie do or other nowadays, usually a speaking engagement at a sportsmen's dinner. Very often I go with my good friend Tim Witherspoon, the great American former world-heavyweight champion. He's a grand lad, is Tim; really down to earth and fun to be around. He lives in the UK now, and Angie and my daughter Carla are good friends with his partner. We meet up with them now and again for boxing dinners and so on.

'Terrible Tim' won the world title twice in the 1980s. A lot of people will remember him for beating Frank Bruno up, when he knocked him out with one of his famous windmill punches. He had a really strange boxing style but it worked for him.

We have a right old laugh, me and Tim. He's got a really great turn of phrase and his Americanisms crack me up. I remember once I was driving him to a do somewhere and one of my mates overtook us. It was a really silly manoeuvre and Tim was shaking his head in astonishment. He turned round to me and said: "Is that guy having a piss?"

What he was actually trying to say, of course, was, "is he taking the piss?", but it came out all wrong. We were howling for days about that one.

25) Screaming Skull

In the summer of 2012 the B-Bad boys had lined me up to fight the Welshman Paul 'The Rage' Pestell at BKB2 in Hinckley, near Leicester.

I wasn't really ready for a bare-knuckle dust-up with anyone, let alone 'The Rage'. I'd put on a bit of timber that year because I hadn't been training properly and I'd been pubbing it too much with The Undertaker. Work got in the way as well, but so did gallons of lager. I'm now a ground worker in deep drainage and have jobs on building sites all over the country. I'm never short of work, which means I'm alright for the dough but I've been taking on fights with a bit of a paunch because I'm not sweating off the pounds at the gym.

Nevertheless, when Andy Topliffe asked me to fight on the B-Bad 2 card I accepted. It was to be held at a secret location on October 27. Andy had lined up 10 fighters for five bare-knuckle bouts, the main event being a UK title fight between Andy 'No Fear' Hillhouse - a thoroughly-scary looking Scot with a Mohican hair cut - and martial-arts specialist Karl 'Lightning Fist' Wing Chung. It would be the first time that a bare-knuckle British title belt had been up for grabs since 1890. Topliffe had arranged the showdown on the back of his B-Bad Promotions label, which is trying to bring the sport back into the open.

Pestell was apparently a handy lad who had put some big names away, but he was still a bit of an unknown quantity and Wing Chung could have been the Karate Kid for all I knew. As it happened, 'The Rage' pulled out, so I was down to fight Hillhouse. I was all geared up for fighting the Tartan terror, knowing that he might have the power to put me away if I didn't land the big left, but he failed to live up to his name and pulled out, so I was down to fight the Kung Fu kid. But then he pulled out too, leaving me and a Geordie guy called James 'Gypsy Boy' McCory to fight for the vacant UK belt. As per usual, my best mate and trainer George 'Screaming Skull' Probert would be in my corner. I love George, and if anyone is completely deserving of their nickname, it's him. I call him Screaming Skull because, despite being one of the most placid men you could wish to meet in the normal course of events, he goes ballistic at any perceived injustice – particularly when it concerns his good mate The Beast. Seriously, when he loses it, it really is a sight to behold. His skin ripples, his skull shakes; his eyes pop out. He's like a cartoon character gone haywire.

'Gorgeous George' has been in my corner at some of my toughest scraps; shared my highs in victory and lows in defeat. He's always had my best interests at heart and I know I could trust him with my life. We've been mates for 20 years, since when I was about 23 and he was 16. My mates tell me that when I'm fighting Skull feels every punch. On one unforgettable occasion he let rip at a boxing promoter because he thought he'd screwed me. I'll not name names here, but this promoter really did get both barrels from The Skull that night. It was the time I was supposed to be having a re-match with Duran in a three-round exhibition in Doncaster. Loads of people, me included, were looking forward to the event but when I got there it turned out Duran didn't have a clue it was happening as he'd only just had a hernia operation and plainly couldn't fight. Jesus, Mary and Joseph, The Skull screamed the place down! He got right up into the promoter's face and gave him the old hairdryer treatment.

Skull pointed at me and bellowed in the guy's face: "That man needs to know what's going off! He's walking around in circles; he doesn't know what's going off!"

I've known George a long time but even I couldn't believe what I was seeing. I was laughing so hard it hurt. The promoter – who's a big lad himself and towered over George – just took it at first but then he started to get angry. One of my guys came over to me and said: "Dave, you better do something here. It looks like it's gonna kick off. He's gonna take our George out."

The thing is, I'd burst my ear drums in a sparring session the day before and I could hardly hear anything. But I could sense that George might be in trouble and when the promoter got wind of this he calmed down, because he knew I wouldn't be able to let it go if my mate was in any kind of danger. Don't get me wrong, he can handle himself, can George. He's not a big lad but he can do a bit, believe me. I can say this with some certainty because I've had a few whacks off him myself down the years. We used to go to York Races once a year with a load of Hemsworth lads, and me and George were the star attraction because of our annual fight on the bus journey back home. We'd get a few beers down us on the way and, suitably refreshed, we'd take a few seats out to make room for our humdinger. Then: BANG!

Skull would crack me one in the chops and we'd start going at it hell for leather. We'd bust each other's noses so bad there'd be blood gushing out all over our clothes, the bus seats and the windows. You can only imagine the state we were in when we got back home, our shirts drenched in blood. The funny thing is, we used to stop off at a pub in Sherburn on the way home and they'd let us in, happily serving us beers, despite the fact that we looked like we'd just walked off the set of a horror movie.

Of course, it's all in good spirits with me and George. We don't make a habit of knocking the shit out of each other; it was just sort of traditional for us to let the blood flow when we went made our annual trip to York Races. Me and George have never had a proper scrap but once I really did hurt him. It was a complete accident but I ended up popping his nose. We were in Hull at the time and I'd just had a do with some guy, so my blood was up. George said something to try to calm me down and I threw a left hook to his body, stopping just short as I always do. Then I threw a right-hook cross to his chin, intending to stop just short again, but this time he'd moved his head down and I caught him clean on the nose. It bust his pecker open and there was blood spurting everywhere. George took a tissue out of his jacket and began wiping the blood off – he always takes a tissue with him when he comes out with me, just in case he cops a pretend one off me that hits the mark by mistake. I was absolutely mortified that I'd hit my best friend and I almost started to cry. To me, he's my little boy and I wouldn't let anyone hurt him, but on this occasion I'd done the job myself. I was depressed all day long.

George took over from James Walker as my trainer when I started bare-knuckling. It was the natural choice as he knew me inside out. I wouldn't feel quite the same going into a bare knuckle without my bosom buddy stood in my corner.

Now some people might think that only a masochist could have a trainer called The Screaming Skull, a favourite sparring partner called Nasty Neil and friends with names like Pyscho, The Clobberer, The Undertaker and The Bull. But names deceive: my guys are the real deal and they're with me for life. You'd go in the trenches with The Clobberer, wage your life on The Undertaker, and you can put the kettle on for Nasty. As for the Screaming Skull, he's a softie at heart, just like me. We have so much in common and I've even managed to get him into Irish folk music! No shit, the Skull will be joining me this spring for the annual Irish folk festival in Holmfirth. Who'd have thought it?

26) Battle on the Straw

The fight was held at a venue called Harry's Place in the centre of Hinckley. I have no idea where they find these places, but find them they do and all credit to the organisers for keeping the bizzes at bay.

So I was back in Leicester again: I've forgotten how many times I've fought in that bloody place. They might as well reserve me a bleeding parking spot out there!

I went down to the fight in the Range Rover with the Skull, The Bull, Psycho, Ashley The Vice, The Clobberer and The Undertaker. Well it was Hallowe'en weekend!

The omens weren't good from the start. We couldn't find a parking place for love nor money and there were all these piss-heads and people dressed as ghouls and goblins out in the street. I remember we stopped the Rover and asked a zombie where Harry's Bar was. The zombie looked at us non-plussed and carried on his way. Further down the street was a group of young lads who looked like they were up to no good. It was only 5.30pm but they were pissed out of their heads already. We saw one of them pull a moony at a group of girls inside a take-away. These lads were shouting and bawling at everybody they passed – it made us wonder what kind of state they'd have been in by the witching hour. To think there were all those heavy lads inside Harry's Place for what was effectively an illegal event, and there wasn't a bit of trouble, yet these louts in the street were at liberty to go around abusing anyone they saw fit. You can say what you want about the knuckle scene, but you'd be much safer at a BKB event than you would on the high street on a Saturday night. That is for sure.

Now if, like us, you're ever lost trying to find a bare-knuckle venue, just look for the shaven heads and big biceps– that's the tell-tale sign that you've reached your destination. We eventually saw the shaven heads stood outside Harry's Place, which was next to a neon-lit Motown bar. Oddly, it was completely empty. To get to Harry's gaff you had to walk through a dark corridor between the

Motown place and a high-street shop. You then walked up two flights of stairs, past a hairdresser's and some locked rooms, inside which was anyone's guess. And there it was: Harry's Place - a cold and dreary room with hardly any décor or soft furnishings to speak of. There were some tables set aside for the VIPs to the left of the large room and a bar in the middle, next to the 'ring', which was marked out by dozens of straw bales. In the far corner of the bar was a mock fireplace and easy chairs where a group of ageing gipsy men and the cloth-cap brigade were huddled together away from the younger crowd, who were gathered around the taps: big, meaty fellas covered in tattoos – and most of them were my crowd! A lot of guys had come down from Hemsworth for the fight and even the Leicester lot, including Mr Platts, Albert Fox and the Bulldog's supporters, had come to support me.

The atmosphere was beginning to sizzle already. You could sense that the punters knew they were in for something special. There were rumours flying about that James Quinn McDonagh and big-time actor Ray Winstone - who apparently loves his bare-knuckling – were on their way. I was more bothered about whether my opponent was gonna turn up or not, and, as the minutes turned to hours and he still hadn't shown, I feared the worst. The first fight was supposed to start at 6pm but it was already gone seven and there was only me and Matt 'Quick Hit' Thorn in the house. If I was on pins waiting for my man - who was supposedly on his way down from Newcastle - then old Quick Hit was a complete bag of nerves and I can't say I blamed him. There's nothing worse than waiting for your man when he's running late.

During those unbearable hours waiting for the other fighters to show, Matt was in among the crowd, shifting from side to side, back and forth, in little staccato bursts: two feet forward, two feet back, a step to the right, a stride to the left; psyching himself into a frenzy, imagining his foe was right there before him. His opponent was still travelling down the motorway from Wales, so, for the time being,

Quick Hit would busy himself by walking up to the big biceps in the crowd, snarling and growling at the lot of 'em.

Good old Quick Hit: he may not be the best boxer in the world and, at 11st, quite light for a bare-knuckler, but he's got the heart of a lion.

The knuckle crowd love Matt for his courage. You tend to see the same faces at the knuckles and they're a very respectful lot, always getting behind the underdog if he shows plenty of heart. But it has to be said, you do get one or two oddballs at the knuckles, usually there on their own. The vast majority of the knuckle crowd are just heavy lads with good hearts, but nobody ever seems to know who these strange ones are, where they come from or how they got tickets. I clocked a few of these types as I whiled away the hours waiting for my man to arrive. After two hours had passed, people were starting to think there might not be a fight night at all.

Two guys from Cage Amateurs UK, which promotes BKB and MMA, were making a DVD of the night and had set their equipment up to video the fights. There was also a shifty-looking freelance journalist with a camera who was doing a piece for a national newspaper – he was looking a tad pissed off, to say the least. Then the big man arrived - Paddy Monaghan, supposedly the best middleweight bare-knuckle boxer there's ever been. They say he's had 114 fights and no losses – now that must take some doing.

Paddy was in his 60s now but looked unbelievably well considering the number of fights he'd had. He turned up in a pin-stripe suit with his wife on his arm and a bonny girl who I think was their daughter. Paddy was such a nice guy and there was not a bit of bravado about him. He must have been wondering why the hell there had been no action yet, but, being a gentleman, he kept his counsel.

The Welshman Seth Jones finally turned up, at which point Quick Hit darted off to the changing rooms. Jones was a mature student at Bangor University in the final year of a law degree. He was a softly-spoken man and looked like he wouldn't say boo to a goose, but I could tell there was a hint of menace in his eyes. He was a small but powerful-looking man with huge arms and rippling muscle. He must have been at least 50 years old but he looked very handy.

Me and Jones were collared by the Cage Amateurs guys for a pre-fight interview along with Andy and Danny Draper, who would be refereeing my fight. Draper helps promote the BKB events and he and Andy were on the sofa telling the Cage Amateurs guys why the sport should be legalised and the things they had been doing to make it more mainstream.

I took my place on the B-Bad sofa and was interviewed by a Kentish lad called Daniel Towers. He was a nice fella and the interview went well, but it was only later, when I watched the B-Bad DVD back at home, that I realised my blue checked flannel shirt clashed horribly with the room's colour scheme. All the way through the interview I couldn't stop thinking about the Geordie boy. Had the fucker ducked out? Was he stuck on the motorway? Or had the zombies got him?

As soon as the cameras stopped rolling I left the interview room and went looking for him, but still he hadn't arrived. People were starting to get fidgety; a lot of people had travelled a long way for this, many of them my people from Hemsworth. Then word got round that he was here. I checked with Andy and he confirmed that the gipsy boy had arrived. I was elated and relieved at the same time.

I knew I would be really up against it even before I saw the lithe, toned, twentysomething McCory stroll in wearing a loose-fitting sleeveless T-shirt and tracksuit bottoms. You see, I knew he went straight down the middle, stood tall and packed a raking punch. By all accounts he also had a very good chin.

But first up were Jones and Quick Hit. By now the old gipsy men and cloth caps had moved away from the snug corner with the mock fireplace to gather round the straw ring reinforced by umpteen shaven heads. Mr Platts and some of the other caps stretched out a foot onto a straw bale as if they were watching cows grazing. The mob was starting to purr now: you can always tell when the bare-knuckle crowd is getting excited about a fight because they speak in hushed tones. It was almost silent when Quick Hit entered the ring in that jolty way of his: two strides hither, two strides thither; one forward, one back. Eyes fixed, ablaze.

I must confess I didn't watch any of the fight - I can never bear to watch others going at it - but I saw it later on the B-Bad DVD and what sticks out in my mind is the way Matt's shoulders tensed up when Jones entered the ring. Quick Hit reared up like a cornered cat in season, adrenal pinballs whizzing round his body. He eyed Jones as the Welsh dragon bounded into the ring with a look of supreme confidence. The thickset Taffy was Cool Hand Luke. It was as if he were apologising to Quick Hit before the bout had even started. I looked over at Paddy Monaghan and wondered what the bare-knuckle king made of this match-up. Quick Hit's heart must have been pounding, bless him.

The ref – who, funnily enough, was Matt's old nemesis Dale Hyde, who'd defeated him at B-Bad 1 – brought the two fighters together. Matt snarled at his opponent but Jones, almost angel-like, simply clasped the palms of his hands together beneath his chin and bowed slightly, like a beefy Buddha: he was gonna come at Quick Hit with a smile. The Welshman was obviously a martial-arts man who knew how to conduct himself.

Quick Hit looked at his man like he was looking into the eyes of his maker. A hush settled on the crowd. The two men danced around each other to begin with, sizing each other up. Then: WHAM! Quick Hit took a blinder on the chin and Jones rattled him with some vicious kidney shots. Matt was hurt already but the crowd willed him to stay with his man. Then Jones - his broad shoulders, bull neck and tree-trunk arms bulging out of his university vest - unleashed a series of hammer blows to the ribs and face that stunned Quick Hit. One screaming body shot seemed to split Matt's rib cage in two. He was down on the bales.

The poor lad was struggling to get up, but, with the crowd urging him on, he managed to get back on his feet as the ref counted him down. You generally have 20 seconds to get back on your feet and ready yourself to fight again in bare-knuckle contests, and Quick Hit just made it in time. He looked rattled, did the lad, but he was a game, fighting man with plenty of heart. He came back at his tormentor with real aggression, but then the ferocious power of the Welshman's punching forced him back to the corner and within seconds he was on his back. It was Jones's body shots that were doing the damage: they were tearing into Quick Hit's torso like carving knives. For those of you who've never been to the knuckles, it's maybe hard to comprehend the sickening crack of a bone-on-bone punch that hits the target without the leather padding of the glove. The glove produces a wispy sound, but a good knuckle shot is more like a clunk, a crack, a whiplash.

The beating that brave Quick Hit was taking was starting to make the crowd a little uneasy. There was real concern for the lad and about what was to come next. He was slumped on a bale again, alone with his thoughts. It wasn't hard to see what was going through his mind: do I carry on and let this man give me a beating or do I just give up? The count was on – Quick Hit got up on 18. He reared up, looked into his maker's eyes again, then nodded to himself and held his hands aloft as if in prayer. The fight was back on.

Within seconds a vicious combination from the Welshman put Quick Hit on his arse again. The killer blow was a fearful clout to Matt's head – he was poleaxed. This time there were no bales to support his fall and he lay motionless on the floor. He was groaning now and there was blood spattered all over his face and chest. But he got up again and chuntered to himself as he wiped blood out of his nose: "Fuck! FUCK!!"

"It's only a bit of blood son," said Hyde.

It seemed only a matter of time before Matt hit the deck again, but, unbelievably, he came back at Jones and actually put him on his arse! To be fair, it was only Jones's momentum as he retreated from a Quick Hit counter-attack that caused him to fall backwards onto the bales, and when he got back up he looked as composed as ever. But old Quick Hit, heartened by his counter-attack, was bobbing and weaving like a good 'un now. Unfortunately, his second wind didn't last long and the inevitable came in the form of a crashing thump that floored him for the fourth time. Matt swore at himself but was up on 17. Within a few seconds the timekeeper signalled the end of the first round. Quick Hit had made it the second round - give that man a medal!

The second phase of the fight didn't last long. Quick Hit pulled his aching bones from the refuge of the bales and came out for the second in slightly-less-spirited style. To be fair to the lad, he'd spent the past 10 minutes having the shit kicked out of him, and his face, arms and chest were drenched in blood. His nostrils must have been caked in the stuff 'cos he was trying to sniff it out. Andy Topliffe asked him if he was alright to carry on, and, to huge cheers from the crowd, he said yes. Marvellous Matt went back at Jones like a man possessed, but the university man simply dropped his shoulders, arched back and, from a back-foot stance, let fly a huge hook that caught Matt right on the sweet spot. You could have heard the crunch a mile away; even the crowd let out a moan as Matt hit the deck. There were some in the crowd urging him to carry on, but others were shouting: "Leave it Matt!"

And, thankfully for Quick Hit and surely all concerned, he didn't manage to beat the count this time. With the fight over, the two men hugged and Matt could be heard telling Jones: "That was a good shot."

Bless old Quick Hit. I've heard he was brought up in care somewhere in Wakefield and found his way into the knuckle game somehow. He's not the greatest fighter in the world but fair play to him for having the bollocks to go on the straw with some seriously brutal guys. I like Quick Hit: he's a lovely guy and he was born with a fighter's heart. I've heard he's won a few bare-knuckles too. Good on you lad.

27) John Merrick II

I knew the fight with the Geordie guy was gonna be a tough one. I'd heard he liked to go straight down the middle, that he was a no-nonsense fighter with a good chin. He was only in his mid-20s, so he had age on his side too.

It had taken McCory six hours to get down from Newcastle. Apparently, the people who were supposed to be giving him a lift let him down, but a mate stepped in at the last minute. They bombed it down the A1 and got there late but just in time. The Gypsy Boy waltzed into the bar with a swagger but the guy was no braggart. He looked like a man who knew his trade and was confident of doing the business. Nothing wrong in that.

In the changing rooms just before the fight, there were loads of people jostling around: the fixers, the fighters, the gamblers and the corner men. Side bets were being placed and payments being discussed. I had a quick word with McCory, who was dressed in black tracksuit bottoms and a green vest. He looked quite lean because of his height but his biceps were huge and his muscles were rippling out of his sleeveless top. He had a typical gipsy look: dark, rugged, unshaven. He said to me that he would shake my hand before the fight and offer me his hand afterwards, win or lose. I had to give this man respect. He seemed a nice enough lad.

I went out first. I was relieved to get the flannel shirt off but didn't feel right in the grandfather vest. The crowed seemed subdued before the first fight - probably because they'd had to wait so long to see some action - but now they were starting to purr. There was real tension and electricity in the air. You got the feeling that the crowd didn't know which way this would go.

The atmosphere at bare-knuckle shows is so different to the buzz at a glove fight: it's much more highly-charged in BKB. For someone like me, who feeds off the super-charged tension of a pre-fight build-up, it's irresistible.

By now the adrenaline rush was fizzing up and down my spine like an unstoppable electric current. I walked between the bales at the far end of the ring and waited. I kicked my legs back and forth, looked down at the floor, alone with my thoughts; waiting, waiting….

There was an odd silence for about 30 seconds and then a huge cheer went up as McCory entered the ring – that was from the gipsy element. The ref called us into the middle. He laid down the rules; we gave each other the nod. McCory asked God to bless me.

We were bang at it right from the off. He caught me with some good jabs within seconds and hit me with a snorter just below the eye, but then I caught him with an even harder one – he didn't flinch. We were trading heavy blows and it was obvious already that the fight wouldn't last long: something would have to give.

McCory sent in a pile-driver that was heading right for my sweet spot but I backed off just in time. We went straight back in at each other and were toe-to-toe again, just the way I like it. But then I noticed blood was beginning to trickle from my nose and my eyes felt swollen. They were bulging out of my head and the fight was only a few minutes' old. I thought, "Bollocks to this", and went back at the Gypsy Boy like a man possessed. I clobbered him with a big left followed by a nice uppercut: he reeled a little but held strong. I got back in close and hammered him with another huge left, but still he kept coming forward, trading blow for blow. The shots were really whizzing in now and the crowd was working itself up into a lather. After one lightning exchange they started clapping us – it was shaping into a really good scrap.

I slugged McCory with a big left to the chin but he took it well. We squared up again, but suddenly I didn't feel right. I could feel the puffed-up flesh around my eyes beginning to obscure my vision. I kept throwing punches and managed to dodge a few bombs, but my vision got worse and all of a sudden the gipsy boy was just a blur. I was practically blind but instinct drove me on. I kept on walking into big shots, trying to find a way through the fog to land a good Joseph and put McCory away. But the fog was growing thicker and I could hear the crowd groan when he threw a big left-right combination that rattled my bones. I didn't see either of them coming because I was staring into my own pink flesh.

McCory's rapier punches hadn't really hurt me – I could take much more of that – but the blurriness of my vision was affecting my co-ordination and made my legs unsteady. I suddenly broke off from him and went down on one knee. The crowd was deathly silent – a lot of them were my people and they weren't used to seeing The Beast go down at will. Even in my sorry state, I could tell what they were thinking: "Is Dave Radford *really* submitting?"

Draper began the count of 20 as The Skull looked at the horrific swelling around my bugged-out eyes and cheekbones, which were jutting out at weird angles. The count reached 16, 17, 18....19......20!

"The boy's out!" cried a gipsy voice.

I was still down on one knee and the swelling was getting worse. Draper looked down on me with a mixture of pity and shock. He had been the Elephant Man when I nailed him in Leicester - now I was John Merrick II!

McCory came straight over to me and shook my hand, just as he had promised in the changing rooms before the fight. I got back on my feet and he gave me a hug. Then something strange happened – there were mutterings inside the ring about the fight continuing.

"I'll fight on," I said to Draper. "I'll try and carry on for another minute. If I can't, you can stop it whether I win or lose."

"Are you sure?" he asked. There was a look of bewilderment in his eyes. "Do you want to fight or not?"

"Yeah, I'll carry on."

"DO you want to fight or not?" he repeated.

"No he fucking doesn't!" came the cry from my corner. It was Georgie boy. He could see that my face was horribly puffed up and I know that George, more than anyone, knows when I can and cannot carry on. He's been with me at so many brutal dust-ups and, as far as I'm concerned, whatever he says, goes. So the fight was over. Draper held McCory's arm aloft and declared him the UK champion. They put the BKB belt around his waist and Paddy Monaghan came over to congratulate him.

The puffiness around my cheeks and eyes was so bad that I was beginning to look like the Marshmallow Man. I looked for all the world like the classic beaten fighter. I could see the looks of concern on people's faces. I was thinking to myself: "If only the missus could see me now!"

I was thinking about my kids, the grandkids, my dad, Gareth, mum. I felt I had let them all down.

It's an odd feeling when you've just been beaten in a fight, and of course I'm not used to getting beaten at the knuckles. In the 10 minutes or so after the fight has ended, you have nothing to say, so your mates do your talking for you. They were swarming all over me after the fight, putting their arms around me, patting me on the back and trying to console me. You could tell they were hurt and also a bit in shock at what they had just seen. They had presumed, as I am sure did all my supporters, that we'd be driving back up the A1 with the BKB belt, ready to give the good news to everyone back home. But it wasn't to be.

Fair play to McCory; he took some big shots off me that night and never flinched. I suppose, when all's said and done, it was what a good knuckle fight is all about: three or four minutes of intense battling, with no quarter given. Also, we'd managed to get a belt on the scene for the first time in 120 years and some publicity in the national press. The sports guys at the tabloids have been trying to get their snouts in the bare-knuckle trough for years. It was inevitable, I suppose, that it was the Sunday Sport, the 'White Van Man's paper', which got in their first. The article ran on a centre spread below a headline which read: 'After two minutes I couldn't see. I was fighting blind!'

Good on the Sunday Sport for having the balls to bring the knuckle game back into the limelight. Their article, which was a brilliant one, featured a triumphant picture of McCory with the UK belt around his waist, and, next to it, was a picture of Yours Truly down on one knee, with the ref counting me down and my mates stood behind me with these really worried looks on their faces. Jesus, Mary and Joseph, my face looked a right bleeding mess.

In a way, I was pleased they used that picture with the 'Fighting Blind' headline because it helped to scotch rumours going around the village that I'd been beaten up. Besides, I like the publicity!

Topliffe was quoted in the article as saying how he was trying to get BKB into the mainstream and how the sport had been misinterpreted as a game for thugs. I knew what The Sport was up to: they were trying to make BKB out to be a real-life Fight Club, the film where Brad Pitt plays this guy who arranges no-holds-barred fights down in basements and cellars. There was nothing wrong with that and it probably helped to sell some papers. Besides, in some ways it is like Fight Club, only less brutal. I have to admit I haven't seen the film all the way through - I'd rather watch a good George Formby movie or a black-and-white weepy. Good old George: he and his ukulele really cheered me up in those two or three weeks after the fight, when I was sitting at home recovering from busted bones and aching limbs. There was no way I could go straight back to work - my face was a right mess. The blood in my cheek had hardened and the swelling took a whole month to go down. I went to the doctor's to get my cheekbones checked out and he told me I'd probably fractured them. Despite the state I was in, I still say that, if my eyes had been alright during the fight, I would have been able to carry on and maybe beat the kid. But my vision went all to cock and I couldn't focus on the target. At one point I couldn't see anything. I was fighting with one eye from the first minute and, when they shut completely, that was it. I'd never missed with so many left hooks as I did against McCory. It was a bad fight for me from the get-go but I've been in tougher scraps where I've been hurt more and still won. Against the Gypsy Boy there were only two punches he threw that did all the damage.

I did a lot of thinking after the fight and decided that it wasn't time to retire just yet. The buzz I got that night, with all my friends around me and the crowd purring, was one you couldn't buy. There's always that buzz around when I'm about to do battle because everyone knows I'll fight my heart out. It's not often they don't get their money's worth when I'm involved: I consider it my job to give them a good night's entertainment.

Even the missus has come round to the fact that she can't stop me doing what I want to do. We've come to a compromise: she says she won't nag me about stopping so long as I prepare correctly for each fight, because then she won't be as worried about me getting my face smashed up again.

There's another person I need to keep off my case - my friend The Clobberer. Before the McCory fight he kept pestering me to train harder.

"What are you doing?" he'd say. "There's only three weeks to go before the fight!"

Craig's always texting me, telling me I'm not training hard enough. He says I'm not doing myself justice. I intend to put that right, Craig.

28) 'I'll fight you in a phone booth'

Fighting on the straw with no gloves is a real man's game, but it's nothing compared to what the fist merchants of the 19th century got up to - they'd fight 'til the cows came home.

I take my hat off to those gentlemen fighters of the late 1800s, not just because they'd slug it out for two or even three hours, but also because they were courteous men of honour.

Bob Fitzsimmons, Jack Welsh and Jem Carney are my favourites. I don't really hero-worship anybody but, if I had to choose from my all-time favourite fighters, Carney would be right up there. He won the English lightweight title in 1884 after beating a guy called Jake Hyams in a 45-round fight that lasted an hour and three-quarters. I think I'd have had to retire after a bout like that, but Carney had loads of 'em!

I've also read a lot about Jack Welch, a gentleman to the core. He took so much hammer during his career that his ears became cauliflower-shaped, but he had the heart of a lion and kept coming back for more. As a mark of respect to the man, I've got his image tattooed on one of my calves.

But Fitzsimmons was in a class of his own, without doubt one of the all-time greats. He was boxing's first three-division world champion, a middleweight who had the upper-body strength to mix it with the heavies. He's in the Guinness Book of Records as the lightest-ever heavyweight world champion. Some say he's the best pound-for-pound boxer there's ever been. He was a Cornishman with a fearsome left hook - they called him The Freckled Wonder. He had Irish blood, like me.

Fitzsimmons and Carney would have taken some beating. Boxing was still in its crude form back then but these two were good with or without the gloves. They were hero-worshipped back in their day but must have been paid peanuts compared with the crazy sums top prize-fighters earn nowadays. What I like about the fighters in those days was the way they conducted themselves. They were the perfect gentlemen and held in high regard by everyone, regardless of class, even by the snobs and toffs who jumped on the boxing bandwagon when the sport became popular. Their behaviour in and out of the ring was impeccable, and seemed to reflect a different way of life, a time when gentlemanliness still meant something – certainly a lot more than it does now.

Maybe I'm old-fashioned but there's something about that era and those Victorian fighters that has always appealed to me. It may seem a bit outdated, but even today I would never dream of swearing in front of a woman, and I'm sure Welsh and Carney would have been just the same. When you think about how some boxers conduct themselves today – all this hype and bravado in the run-up to a big fight on TV – it's all a sham really; just a cheap way of boosting viewing figures and putting more pennies in their purse. And then I look around at all these arse-holes causing havoc in town centres on a Friday and Saturday night. That's fist-fighting in its lowest form: most of these guys are just bullies, pure thugs and nothing more.

People can say what they want about the bare-knuckle scene, but I've never met anyone on the scene who I regard as a bully. Yes, the fist game in its rawest form can be brutal and horrid. Down the years I've fought in some horrible places and some of the punters are extremely dangerous men, but Topliffe and the B-Bad movement are starting to alter the image of the sport. The last time they staged a show they even managed to get a proper ring - no straw bales in sight.

Now I'm a small-town lad and I hardly leave my village except for work, but all the darkness and shadiness that goes with a knuckle fight is like water off a duck's back to me. You see, I know that once the dust settles and it's just me and the other guy with the fists up, I'm more than capable of doing the business. Sometimes I just know I'm going to put the other guy down. I bet Fitzsimmons used to get that feeling every time he fought. Please don't mistake my confidence for arrogance. I'm a modest man and the only thing I can say for certain is that I was born with a fighter's heart. I was never a man of the street like Tyson or a brawler like Duran: it's all heart and a decent left hook with me. I don't even pretend to be a master of the ring. I'm only half-joking when I say I'd rather fight in a phone box than a field or in The Cage. A straight, toe-to-toe fight with no movement forward, back or sideward for either fighter would be ideal for me. I like to get right in at my man's chest, as near to his heart as possible so I can hear it beat; get right inside him so I can feel his breath. Stick to him like a limpet, alter his breathing patterns. Suffocate him like a giant mollusc.

There used to be an old form of knuckle boxing called Irish Stand Down which would have suited me down to the ground. It was basically fist-fighting stripped down to its purest form. The fighters weren't allowed to move – they just stood there throwing punches at each other until one of them dropped. It was popular in the Irish ghettos of the United States in the 1800s but died out at the end of the century as gloved boxing began to take over. Pity that.

Like the old Stand Down fighters of the ghettos, I have a basic sort of boxing style and I've never tried to change it one bit. I never watch videos of other boxers or my opponents before a fight. Why should I? I always fight the same way anyway, no matter who I'm facing. I change my style for no-one. If they outbox me, fair enough. It may have lost me a few bouts down the years, but as long as I've had a good scrap and enjoyed it, so what? Me and my mates have a saying: "Win or lose, drink some booze; if you draw, drink some more!"

It's a nice little rhyme and it pretty much sums up my attitude to the sport, which changed after I had the accident. I really did fall out of love with the game. I stopped watching fights on TV and missed a whole generation of top fighters in what was supposed to be a new golden age for the sport. Now I'm sure that guys like Ricky Hatton, Manny

Pacquiao, Calzaghe and Floyd Mayweather were, and in some cases still are, brilliant boxers, but I couldn't judge because I've never seen any of them fight. They say Amir Khan is one of the best - I wouldn't have a clue. I think I've seen him on TV a couple of times when they've shown one of his fights in the pub, but I just glance up at the screen a few times and that's it – doesn't interest me.

To think that I was so in love with the game then I turned my back on it after a ton of metal fell on me and my workmate John. He invited me to his wedding recently. It meant so much to me that I turned down a bare-knuckle fight that was scheduled for the same day. To be honest, it was nice to go to a wedding for once without having cuts and bruises all over my face. It's not easy to scrub up well when you look like you've just had an argument with a mincing machine.

29) My Little Man

No matter how many times I get my head battered in a scrap, it comes nowhere near to the pain I still feel at the loss of my two angels in the sky. Mum and Gareth are with me every time I step into the ring. If only they could tell me to stop, I'd stop. Without mum's guidance, am I still punishing myself for her absence? The mind suffers, the fight provides the cure. Afterwards, the body cries out.

Mum and Gareth are buried at Hemsworth Cemetery. I still can't go there without bursting out.

Nowadays it's more painful to visit Gareth's grave than mum's because of the way he died, and, because it was relatively recently, the emotions are still raw. I always go alone - I won't even go up there with my daughters or the missus because I know I'll burst into tears. I'll have a chat with mum about the old days. My memory is shocking but there are some things I'll never forget. It's mainly just little things and I keep them to myself. She called me "my little man": I was her blue-eyed boy. Even up to my early twenties she'd put me on her knee for a laugh, pretend to get my wind up like I was a little baby. My abiding memory of her is sat next to the fireplace, smoking and tapping her ash into the fire.

I was so proud when I came back home from my very first shift and she asked me how it went. I was only 16 and it felt great to be able to show her that her "little man" was now a working man. But I was still a mummy's boy – always was. Mum was such a caring mother and my dad, though he had a soft side to him, was the man of the house. He was how a dad should be and my mum was how a mother should be: I had the perfect upbringing and the ideal family home.

Dad never hit any of his kids – he left it to mum to give us a clip round the ear when we deserved it. He was a grafter, my old fella; worked at the pit then went to the gas board digging up roads and what have you. Mum was an auxiliary nurse at South Moor Road Hospital in Hemsworth – the caring profession was her natural calling. She worked a lot of night shifts and would come home at seven o'clock in the morning to get us kids off to school. She started getting ill when her dad was bad. She would get home from work, get my dad's tea ready for when he got home from his shift, then shoot off to see my granddad to look after him. Then she'd be back at work for the night shift. It was just too much for her and I'm convinced that's why she died of heart failure.

In the space of two weeks in January 1992, when I was just 21 years old, I lost my granddad (my dad's dad) on the 18th, my mum on the 27th and my other granddad on the 31st. They were all in hospital at the same time and none of them came out. It was an awful time for the family and I was in bits. I was in and out of the hospital every day for three weeks, sometimes staying with mum all night. My dad's dad was the first to go and we tried to keep it quiet from mum so as not to upset her as she fought for her own life. I remember her lying in her hospital bed and asking my dad how his dad was. We told her he was fine but then dad couldn't hold it back anymore and broke down in tears. I remember thinking how strange it was to see my dad burst out like that – it was the first time we'd ever seen him cry. And there was mum, caring as always despite the immense pain she must have been in, comforting dad from her bed. She looked alright to me so I never thought she was gonna die. But, about a week after my granddad passed away, she took a bad turn and all her organs failed. The hospital staff told us she wouldn't make it through the night.

My mum and granddad dying was the first time I'd lost anybody close to me. Losing mum was like the end of the world for me. We were there by her bedside when it happened, holding her hand and talking to her. While everyone was sobbing their eyes out, I took myself to one side and began smashing my face to bits with my fists. I just couldn't accept what had happened.

157

There have been other times – though, thankfully, not many – when I've literally beaten myself to a pulp because I'm in a situation I cannot accept. There was one such occasion, just after the death of our Gareth, when I lost it completely in a local pub. I was feeling very down at the time and had gone out with our Becky to relax and have a quiet chat, but just about everybody I knew was coming up to me with *their* problems. They poured their heart out to me because they knew I would do anything for the ones I held dear. But on this particular occasion I'd simply had enough, so I picked up a pool cue and smashed it on my face, really hard, again and again and again, until it smashed to pieces. As bits of splintered wood sprayed everywhere, I shouted to no-one in particular: "Why does everyone always come to me with their problems? I've got enough on!"

I was testing myself to see if the hurt I was causing myself physically could be any more than the pain I was feeling inside over Gareth, but it didn't come anywhere near. I barely felt a thing, in fact the pool cue came off worse than me! It was lying there in pieces, crying on the floor – another victim of the Abominable Beast.

30) The Devil's Trident

I'm a walking contradiction: I love to fight but I know it's a mug's game. I'm also fully aware that what I do is fundamentally wrong - but I bet the things you like the most are those you know you shouldn't be doing.

An alcoholic will drink all day knowing that the stuff he lives for will probably kill him. Boxing, for me, is no different. I've never been into drugs and I like my drink but don't depend on it. The fist game, on the other hand, is something I can't do without.

My memory is fading but I still want more. I told everybody I knew and cared about that 2012 would be my last in the fight game. I actually announced my 'retirement' to thousands of my supporters after the exhibition fight with Benn. I clutched the microphone and told them enough was enough. And I meant it too.

But then came the McCory fight and everything changed. I couldn't go out on a defeat so I decided to go for The UK Shield five months later. And then I thought, 'why not go on for another five years?'

I just think that, at the time, I was kidding myself that I could retire. Did I really think I could just step out of the ring, hang up the gloves and call it a day like I was giving up a milk round? Anybody who has ever been serious about their sporting life knows that this is not an easy thing to do. I'm no football fan, but I know that George Best was never the same when he packed in soccer and it was probably his undoing, maybe more so than the booze. Let's face it, my head's fucked, my knees are fucked and my hands are in a shocking state. Sorry for repeated use of the 'f' word, but, in this instance, it's unavoidable. So is the fact that my pride won't let me retire just yet.

I stand true to what I said about not caring whether I win or lose so long as I've had a good scrap, but against the Geordie boy I didn't do myself justice and I can't close the book like that. I didn't train, I was out of shape; I was wearing a grandfather vest for Christ's sake!

People say I'm mad for carrying on when my bones are all busted and the memory is fading. It's got to the stage now where, if I put something down at work – one of my tools, say – I have to ask a mate to keep an eye on them for me until I come back. Even if I just nip to the loo for two minutes, I could easily forget where I've left my stuff.

Driving is the worst – I can get lost even before I leave the village. I've been driving out to Holmfirth on a regular basis for the past 15 years; must have made hundreds of journeys there, but recently I've been losing my bearings before the trip has barely started. Sometimes I can't remember which road to take out of Hemsworth. One of the most confusing things for me is when I come to a fork in the road – it's like the devil's trident. There are times when I don't have a clue which lane to get in. It's pretty frightening, let me tell you.

Of course I do have days of clarity, when the memory comes flooding back, but there are others when the mist is so thick I even struggle to remember the names of people I see on a regular basis. The missus worries terribly about me; so do my kids. I've got six grandchildren now and I want to be a fantastic grandfather to them. I love them all dearly, so why do I carry on fighting? It's not an easy question.

Do I worry about my health? Well yes, of course, but I'm also worried about my mental state if I never go back in the ring. What would I do on a Sunday morning if me and The Clobberer weren't beating the hell out of each other? What would replace the buzz of the cellar fights with Nasty Neil? There's gonna be a vacuum somewhere down the line and I get the feeling my head would be filled with all kinds of dark thoughts and disturbing questions.

Some people must think I'm reckless. The truth is, I'm simply addicted to a sport which comes with a health warning. Nobody wants to get their head beaten out of shape and their memory obliterated. I don't do what I do to destroy my brain and body. I may go to the gym and let The Clobberer beat the crap out of me; might purge myself by taking it to the limits with Nasty Neil down in the cellar, but

I'm no nut job. In fact, just recently, I decided it was finally time to do something about the memory thing. The incident that spurred me into action was a slightly embarrassing one and it finally convinced me that it was time to go and see a doctor. I'd just dropped a mate off after work and was supposed to be picking him straight back up again, but when I drove past his house 10 minutes later it completely slipped my mind. I cruised straight on past his gaff whistling along to a Tony Bennett tune, not a care in the world. He rang me up later on and asked me where the hell I was – I couldn't believe I'd forgotten. I was so ashamed.

The next day I rang the doctor's first thing and arranged an appointment. They gave me an appointment for the following week and prescribed some tablets that are supposed to help your memory. I was quite pleased with myself for finally doing something about it. I'm not sure the tablets are doing much good though.

With my memory being like it is, I know you have to draw a line somewhere. I am also fully aware that there's only so much punishment you can take before Messrs Parkinson and Alzheimer come knocking on the door. I don't want to end up a shivering wreck, but I also know what I can't do without. We've all heard the horror stories about fighters who go on longer than is good for them; about those who take it that one or two bouts too far. Ali is the most obvious example and it proves that even The Greatest is not immune from the sport's lurking dangers. I don't want to end up like Ali, poor guy. He should be basking in the glow of the greatest boxing career there's ever been, but instead he's a shell of the man he once was, trapped in his own body and in constant pain. That's no way to live – it should never have been that way for him.

I know an ex-fighter who went on for years; didn't stop even when everybody was telling him to end the show. He fought lots of really tough bouts and the fights only got tougher the older he became. His memory is shot now and it's getting worse by the day. Does he regret going on for too long? I forgot to ask.

31) Once More Unto The Breach

My rematch with McCory was set for June 15, 2013. The bare-knuckle crowd had been waiting for this one ever since our first tussle six months earlier.

The venue was the same shady bar in Leicester where I'd fought Danny Draper in April 2012. At least this time there would be some form of canvas instead of a rock-hard floor, and there would be a ring of straw bales.

We took about 30 lads with us for the fight. In the weeks leading up to the show, everybody was prepping me up and telling me that this time I would beat the guy. But I knew that deep down they were as scared as hell.

They had seen what McCory had done in the first fight and knew that this time I was going into the rematch with shattered bones and dodgy eyes that could swell up with just one good shot.

I could see real fear in their eyes, though none of them let on that they were worried for me. They feared that I would get seriously hurt and that, with my pride, I'd fight to the bitter end no matter how bad the damage.

Some of my mates told me they wouldn't be turning up for the McCory fight unless I put the training in beforehand. They said it was ridiculous that I should be fighting guys 20 years younger than me after all these years taking on the bruisers of the bare-knuckle pit.

June 15 was a swelteringly-hot day. When we walked into the bar it was like an oven. The place was chock full of heavies and the atmosphere was stifling.

As per usual at the knuckles, we were 'greeted' by a posse of middle-aged gipsy blokes at the entrance, not all of them friendly.

Once inside, I walked straight over to the ring and my heart sank a little. The ring was small, not nearly as big as I'd imagined and wouldn't give me the room for manoeuvre that I was banking on to work round McCory's big shots. I had planned to box the guy, but the size of the ring meant I would have to go straight down the middle again, as I did in the first match. But I had a few other tricks up my sleeve for this one and I knew that this time it would be a lot different to the first fight.

Dozens of my supporters had travelled to Leicester for this, the fourth show of the B-Bad series – and the one I intended to make my last. There were four or five fights on the card and in the first bout a young ruffian called Ross 'Youngblood' McChittock hammered his opponent. The huge crowd – mainly big, hulking fellas with a few glamour girls tossed into the mix – were in a boisterous mood.

My lot - some of them wearing 'Team Radford' T-shirts - looked nervous, especially when McCory waltzed in. He looked like a different bloke to the guy I fought in the first UK title bout. He was much bulkier, with a full-on beard and a paunch. But, in many ways, he looked a lot meaner, tougher, stronger. We'd heard he'd moved up through the weights and been fighting some of the heavies on the glove scene.

He'd come to the fight with a few of his Geordie mates and a bearded guy I presumed was his dad. They went straight to a corner and McCory, wearing a blue superman T-shirt, started his shadow-boxing routine: a worrying sight for Team Radford- the man was clearly in the zone.

My mates didn't like what they saw but I didn't even look at the boy, and he didn't once look at me. There would have been nothing for him to go on anyway: I was happy mingling with the crowd, having a laugh and a joke; totally relaxed and looking forward to the scrap.

I was having a chat with my cousin Alan - who was at his first-ever bare-knuckle show and looked a tad nervous - when Topliffe sidled up to me and said I was up next. I lugged my duffle bag over to the far end of the bar and put my trainers and white sleeveless vest on, then the knee strap. I pushed my way through the heaving crowd to the straw bales and tight ring. McCory followed me in. The crowd erupted.

They were stood around the bales, shoulder-to-shoulder. I inched past Mr Platts wearing his trademark cloth cap, one foot on the bales.

Topliffe, huge beads of sweat dripping from his forehead, brought us into the centre of the ring and gave us the lowdown on a good, clean fight.

Me and James tapped knuckles and broke off. The roar went up.

"Fight!" shouted Topliffe.

We were bang at it from the start, slapping thunderous shots into each other's cheekbones, eyes and stomach. I soon got on top, sending some proper bone-crunchers into McCory's nose, ribs and temple. He replied with two rockets that smacked into my phizzog: the crowd went berserk.

Just like in the first fight, we came in close and stuck to each other like limpets. We were trading body punches that would have taken the wind out of a horse.

I finally managed to unglue myself from his sticky sweat and sent in two hammer blows to his chin which made a sort of snapping noise. He reeled a little - I knew he felt those two.

I drove into him with a vicious combination and my guys went wild. Then the gipsy boy came back with two or three sledgehammers driven into my chest and arms.

Then: WHAM!

He crashed two thunder-slaps into my smiler and I heard a couple of girls shriek. The blows stung but I stayed my ground and went back in close, snuggling right up to his heart. The sweat was making his Superman shirt cling to his chest and I could taste his perspiration.

I managed to pull away from him and peppered him with three or four scuds that shook him.

Then came the barrage I was planning from word go.

BANG! A thunderbolt to the ribs.

BOOM! A vicious uppercut to the chin.

BOP! A Joseph special.

McCory baulked, trying to get his breath, but I was all over him like a swarm of bees. I cracked a left-right combination into his face that stunned him. He was starting to look a bit ragged and my corner was going wild. Then

Topliffe stepped in and called a break.

My guys went mad and boos echoed round the room. None of us were expecting rounds. It gave McCory time to get a breather and regain his composure.

So there I was, back in my corner getting my forehead doused by the Skull, but the heat was so intense I grabbed the bottle of water and poured it all over my body. The lads were saying I had taken the round easily and should do exactly the same in the second.

I left my corner with the Skull bellowing instructions and my mates' cries of support ringing in my lug-hole.

McCory waited in the middle, looking a bit more ruffled than he did in the first fight. His cheekbones were slightly askew, his eyes were puffy and his nose a bit twisted. He knew he'd met the real Dave Radford this time.

I was ready to charge back into him with another heavy combination but he got there first and steamed straight into me with two howitzer blasts to the ribs and forehead, then fired two scuds into my stomach and chest. He'd got his breath back.

I came back at him with a powerful combination and, after landing the Big Left, I felt him wobble slightly as he reeled back towards his supporters in the gipsy end.

He gathered himself, huffed, then nailed me with a big right: I felt the rake of his knuckles buried deep inside my skull. His guys went wild and then erupted again when he tagged me with a left. I lost my balance and slipped on a pool of blood. Topliffe called a temporary halt to proceedings as someone got a brush and mopped up the blood.

Then off it went again: BIFF! BANG! BONG!

By now I could taste McCory's blood, feel his sweat. I heard the pounding of his heart.

We were slugging each other with huge body shots and throwing bombs at each other's chins which would have floored lesser men.

I was on top again by the end of the round, so when Topliffe called for another break it pissed my guys off no end. They let him know what they thought - particularly The Clobberer, who was stood on a table next to a journalist, shouting himself hoarse. He barked at Topliffe, calling him this and that for breaking up the fight.

I was in the corner again getting water poured over my scorching forehead and being offered words of advice from all and sundry.

"Show him Joseph, Dave."

"Let Herbert go!"

"The guy's gone Dave - you can take him."

Third round.

McCory's blue Superman T-shirt is drenched in blood. His nose looks broken; his cheekbones too.

He's throwing bombs at my eyes and cheekbones but I've got them covered with my hands, always there by the side of my face when we're up close. The hands take the blows to protect my face: they're so swollen they must be broken.

I'm going straight down the middle again as I knew I'd have to in this tiny bear pit with little oxygen to breathe. The air is thick, stifling; the crowd hysterical. My heart thumps, my lungs pound, and McCory's crashing one scything blow after another into my temple.

But then I rock him with two haymakers as my hands scream with pain.

SMACK!

I jolt him with a crack to the side of the head and sense that maybe the time is nigh. I follow up with a heavy combination of left and rights which trouble him greatly. His breathing is laboured and the man looks spent. But this is James McCory: he doesn't go down. He wangs one back into my mush that strikes me like a whiplash. I send one back that takes the wind out of him. He crashes one into my solar plexus; I jab a razor fist into his rib cage. We're throwing everything at each other - the fight has gone primitive. Both of us are wilting. My legs are turning to jelly and it's hard to breathe in here. I can sense that old swelling of the eyes again.

We both know that something has to give. We're on the

brink. And then the bell goes.

I'm in the corner again. Bottled water is dripping down my brow onto my aching back and shoulders. Every ounce of my body is throbbing. My eyes sting.

I'm trying to take in gulps of air as The Skull delivers instructions. My guys still believe I can do it.

We're back in the middle and touching hands again. We break off. He comes in.

BANG!

He's pounding me again. I draw him in. I send three concrete blasts into his midriff, cheek and eye sockets. They're proper big shots for a tired man but the gipsy boy remains strong.

I hear the unmistakable rasp of The Clobberer's burnt-out voice: "Come on, baby!".

"You've got him Dave!" shouts my corner as I make my final charge.

WHAM! BAM! BAM!

He's reeling again but stays upright. I've hurt him. His face is puffy. The punters are going nuts - but the big man clings on. Then comes the moment: he's just copped a load of Beast specials and he's smiling!

He looks over at my boys, shakes his head and, with a broad grin, holds his arms aloft in triumph. He knows he's got it now. He can sense my strength is draining. His title is safe.

Back in I go - we're taking this to The End. My lungs are heaving. The blood runs rings around my eyes, squirts from my nose. I'm in the half-light again and the boogey man's there.

"One more time," I tell myself. "One more time."

But he's just a blur now. Strange, muffled noises seep into the ring from the 'outside'. My eyes have gone and the time has come. I shake the man's hand and say well done. It's over.

A big roar goes up from the crowd; applause ripples round the room. The whole place shudders. There are murmurings. It's like the aftermath of a car crash.

The people knew it was a special fight and they could say they were there to witness it. Everything else that comes afterwards must be a footnote.

Everyone was of the same opinion: if that match had come down to points I'd have won. And who knows what might have happened if I had managed to land a proper upper cut? But with one, possibly two, broken hands, that was impossible. I had to let my hands take the heat to protect my head.

My strategy against James had worked but the younger man came through because he had age on his side. My aim was to protect the broken cheekbones and shattered eyes. My hands were so swollen after the fight I could barely hold a knife and fork.

But there was no Elephant Man this time: apart from the broken hands, all I ended up with was a fractured left eye socket. I didn't even bother going to the hospital: I taped my hands up myself and went straight back to work.

McCory went back to Newcastle with a broken nose and fractured cheekbone. He earned his title the hard way and it will take a good man to take it off him. It won't be me because I'm not doing any more B-Bads.

The day after the fight I gathered all my friends and family together for a drink at the George and Dragon to celebrate what I thought had been my last fight.

All the talk was about the best fight that any of them had ever seen. That was good enough for me: all I ever wanted to do was make my family proud and give my mates something to cheer about.

We toasted the gipsy boy, raised our glasses and gave the nod. It was time to get pissed.

The Sunday Sport ran a double-page feature on my first clash with McCory, which the Geordie man won after my eyes swelled up beyond recognition.

Me and the Dark Destroyer trading blows at Rumble in the Park

'The Dog' about to enter the ring before the Benn fight in Hemsworth.

Me and Angie with middleweight legends Roberto Duran (left) and Thomas 'The Hitman' Hearns.

With former middleweight world champ Steve Collins. The man is a true gentleman and a good friend.

Beauties and The Beast: Sharing an intimate moment with Shannon and Buddy, my beautiful grandchildren.

Having a laugh with my 'tablets' Carla and Becky on a trip to the seaside.

With Angie and the 'Glamour Twins' Becky and Carla on a night out.

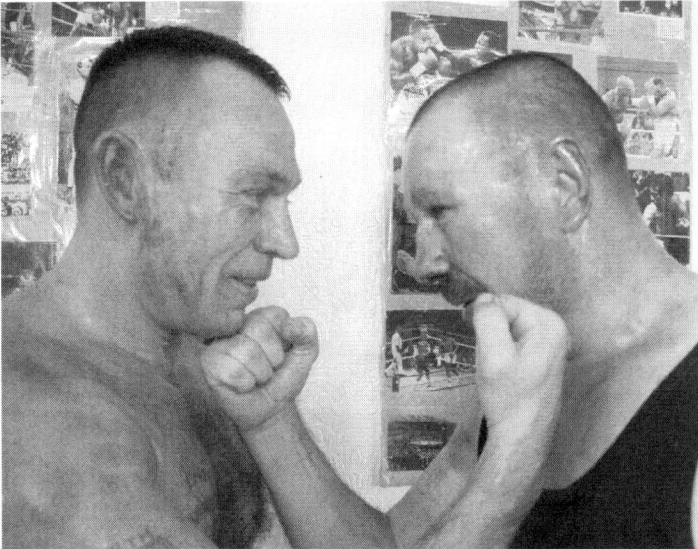

Blood brothers: Me and The Clobberer after a Sunday session at the gym.

At some do or other with 'Terrible' Tim Witherspoon and David Platts.

The Beast and 'Iron Mike'.

From left: Our Carla, Nigel 'The Dark Destroyer' Benn, Becky and Ryan 'The Undertaker' Vincent with Yours Truly at Rumble in the Park.

Me with Cloud, our beloved Weirmaraner. I loved that pesky pooch!

Battling on the straw with James 'Gypsy Boy' McCory at B-Bad 2 in Hinckley. October 27, 2012. I caught McCory with some beauties but I was fighting blind and had to retire.

They must be disciplined!: Making a forceful point to somebody or other just before the first McCory fight. Cor blimey, did I look angry!

My shot at the UK bare-knuckle title comes to an end as I go down on one knee.

Me and the old man.

The aftermath of my first fight with McCory. That boy ruined my looks!

Me with (from left) bare-knuckle legend James Quinn McDonagh and my good friends Craig 'The Clobberer' Smith (second from left) and Ryan 'The Undertaker' Vincent, at a boxing promo event for the big match-up between Roy Jones Junior and Steve Collins.

The Beast with Ryan 'The Undertaker' Vincent (centre) and superman James 'Gypsy Boy' McCory after our second titanic duel in Leicester.

Me and McCory looked like we'd fought a war after our brutal rematch.

Afterword: Beware Greeks Bearing Gifts

The spring and summer of of 2013 was a helter-skelter of good news, bad news and some downright weird news.

I saw my youngest daughter get hitched, was told by my doctor that my eye sockets and cheekbones were in a shocking state, and received a message from a Greek college professor challenging me to a no-holds-barred bare-knuckle scrap for big bucks!

The Greek college boff sent me a message on what I would call my unofficial Dave Radford Facebook page, which was kindly set up for me by my mates without me knowing.

To cut a long story short, this Greek university lecturer from Athens, who also happened to be built like a brick shit house, asked me if I would like to fight him in a few bare-knuckle scraps. He said he'd seen some of my fights on the internet and liked my style. That was weird enough, but it got better: he said he wanted maybe half a dozen 'anything-goes' fights with me – and would pay me at least fifty grand for each fight! What's more, he said he'd come to the UK to fight me in a field somewhere, with no-one else around, until one of us gets sparked out.

The Greek, who shall remain anonymous, said he intended to come over in June or July and stay for about six weeks. During that time, he wanted at least two fights with me: a straight, stand-up bare-knuckle and a no-holds-barred scrap involving elbows, knees, head-butts and groin strikes: 'dirty boxing', as it's known in the business.

I saw a picture of the guy on his Facebook page and from the neck up he looked like what he said he was: a computer nerd and university lecturer. But from the neck down he was a proper beef cake: all rippling muscle, toned pecs and hard, tight arms.

In our online chat he told me he had made some serious money after inventing two computer games that went global. I must admit, it all seemed very strange but I was just thinking about all that dosh – FIFTY GRAND PER FIGHT!

I could retire on that, or at least take a year or two off work. I seriously thought it was going to be my retirement fight - my big pay day at last.

I've never earned more than 18 grand for any one fight – not even for the tussle with Duran - and then all of a sudden this Greek college boffin appears out of nowhere and offers me more money than I've ever dreamt of!

But then the alarm bells started ringing, first when he asked me if I'd ever hit anyone in the groin during a fight. I told him I'd never hit anyone in the groin because that way it would be over too quickly: I liked to trade blows.

But the Nutty Professor was still insisting he wanted a no-holds-barred fight including groin shots and a style of fighting which was last seen in the Irish ghettos of America 150 years ago. He wanted us to stand toe-to-toe and take it in turns to throw pile-drivers at each other: he would hit me with three or four head-and-body combinations, then I'd do the same to him, and so on and so forth until one of us can take no more.

"We fight to the end," is how he put it on the net.

He wanted us to carry on until one of us was unconscious. He talked about fighting beside a lake at night with car lights trained on us, but what really set my suspicions soaring was when he asked me to send him a picture of my naked upper torso. That's when I began to strongly suspect that the Greek's intentions were less than honourable and that he might in fact be feeding his own perverse desires.

When I checked out his Facebook page again he'd deactivated his account: he was obviously either a fraud or he had chickened out. The thought of all that wonga set me drooling, but it was for the best that 'Beast Versus Greek' never materialised. Don't get me wrong, if the guy had been genuine I'd have fought him on Mount Olympus – but I'll never know whether he was a fake or a pussy who just got scared.

The Greek Myth disappeared into the ether but I had more pressing matters at home. I got a call from Andy Booker asking me to act as peacemaker for a sportsmen's dinner to

promote the grudge match between my old mate Steve
Collins, the ex-WBO middleweight and super middleweight
world champion, and American legend Roy Jones Junior,
who held four world titles in his prime. To everyone's
surprise, the two of them had come out of retirement for one
last blast, both well into their 40s. Apparently, they wanted
to settle their 15-year grudge because they never got to meet
each other when they were knocking the shit out of everyone
else. In their heyday, Collins and Jones were pretty much
unbeatable on the canvas and it's just a pity that they never
got in the ring together for what would have been a titanic
duel. Actually, they nearly did get it on back in the 90s, but
it didn't happen for one reason or another despite Collins
saying he would fight Jones "in a phone box in front of two
men and a dog".

The fight will be held somewhere in the UK later this year
and I wouldn't like to call it. Neither of them has fought in
ages – Collins' last appearance in the ring was 16 years ago.
I'll be rooting for my Irish friend, of course, but at the
promotion event in Doncaster I had to be Mr Neutral
because me and James Quinn McDonagh had been tasked to
keep the peace between the two of them. Me and James
were sat at the top table between Collins and Jones Junior,
knowing that we'd have to step in if anything kicked off. To
say Steve and Jones Junior were supposed to hate each
other, they got on fine and The Beast could relax and enjoy
his evening without any mither. Meeting James for the first
time was an added bonus – a smashing bloke.

And so on to my third surprise: I was being head-hunted
by a film company making an international movie! No shit:
a production company called Emu Films had contacted my
local paper asking if they knew how to get hold of me. They
said they wanted me to audition for a part in a film set in the
north. They were looking for a hard man to play the lead
role and I was on the list. Apparently, they'd seen me
fighting on Youtube and knew I had a book coming out.
They got in touch with me and said they wanted me to
audition for the role of a minder, the protector of an Asian

girl called Laila who runs away from her family because she wants to marry a white guy. Her brother and his hoods go looking for her in the badlands of West Yorkshire and it would be the minder's job to try to save her life. The film was called Catch Me Daddy, based on a true story which was all over the national papers at the time. Apparently, the director liked to work with non-actors and liked the look of me. They asked me to the auditions in Manchester and I went over with Skull. I thought they went really well considering it was my first stab at the acting game. There was about a dozen other candidates there for the audition; all big, burly fellas. The casting crew gave us various set-pieces to work on but everything was totally improvised. They gave us a few scenarios but no script, and told us to act as we would in real life. They were using various tricks to cause some kind of off-the-cuff reaction from us. In one scene, me and this Asian guy bet each other £20 on a game of pool. He wins and trouble flares – well they did say act natural!

I went ballistic, kicking a chair over and threatening to cave the guy's head in. He thought it was all part of the act, but he didn't know just how close he'd come to getting a genuine Beast Special right in the chops.

The Skull was convinced I'd get the part. He said all I needed to do was act like Dave Radford and it was mine. As it happened, I missed out on the lead role because of my age, but I got a bit part, which was still no mean feat considering that this film was going out on general release and would be shown to an international audience.

I play a bloke just back from work, with his fluorescent builder's jacket on, waiting for his missus to get her hair done at the hairdresser's when the news comes on the radio about the disappearance of this Asian girl. They told me to say the first thing that came into my head, so I said: "Jesus, what's the world coming to?"

I thought that was a good 'un, but they got me to change it to: "There's no sense in it."

You'll never guess who played my missus - it was my

missus! We drove over to Todmorden in the Pennines to start filming at 6.30am – it lasted 12 hours. Angie was delighted to get a part. The only thing she wasn't too happy about was that the woman playing the hairdresser actually cut bits of her hair out.

As for me, I'm starting to get the acting bug big time. After getting my first taste of the luvvie world, I've now decided to go for a part as an extra in Hollyoaks, the northern soap which our Becky loves. It'll be a walk-on scene as a policeman.

There's a guy in Hemsworth I know who plays extras in the soap and he's told me it's nailed on. Becky has long been a Hollyoaks fan so I'm gonna surprise her and not tell her anything, just watch her face when her old man appears in a bobby's uniform on her favourite soap. Imagine that: Dave Radford as a copper! They've asked me once before to play a policeman but I turned it down because I didn't want to play a cop. But I suppose it's about time I donned that blue uniform after all the times I've helped the police out with their enquiries!

My Hollyoaks mate has told me I'll have to have a shave before I go in front of the cameras. I've told him there's no problem there: The Beast knows how to scrub up when he has to. And who knows? Maybe one day I might even get on Emmerdale and get the chance to knock that twat Cain Dingle all over the place, which I've always wanted to do. Dawg!

Joking aside, it'd be lovely to get my mush on TV. After all the broken bones, busted noses and battered shins I've had down the years, it'd be nice to get some exposure on television without having to risk my looks. I don't want to be sat in a pub in my old age, with a boxer's nose and marks all over my face, and people thinking I was just another fighter who'd had a few bare-knuckle scraps. I may never get my shot at the big time, but I'll never stop trying.

Life is full of ups and downs but you just have to keep on battling. We all have our lows and our heartaches from time to time, but it doesn't matter how many times you stumble and fall, it's how many times you get back up that counts. There have been times when I've been so down in the trough it was difficult to see how I would get back out. But I did, and although I still have periods when the Black Dog shows its beastly face, I always try to look to the positive and never dwell on things too much.

No-one's got it easy. Even my old mate Duran has had his fair share of life's nasty little tricks. He finally retired from the ring in 2002, at the age of 50, after a bad car accident in Argentina left him needing life-saving surgery. In that same year he'd been named by The Ring magazine as the fifth greatest fighter of the past 80 years and the 28th greatest puncher of all time.

But life has no respect for reputations: Duran found this out when his five world-title belts were nicked from his house in Panama in a robbery allegedly staged by his brother-in-law, who was accused of giving them to a seller of sports memorabilia, who allegedly sold them on as stolen goods before he was caught by FBI agents.

So there you have it: even the greatest are not safe from life's many pitfalls. I have a big hand in my favour of course - my shining lights Angie, Carla and Becky. Our Becky got married in March and it was one of the proudest moments of my life. When I went to see her getting her wedding dress on I burst out crying on the spot, then I burst out again when I walked her down the aisle. The waterworks come on so easily with me.

I was so proud to be giving her away that day. My son-in-law Aaron is a smashing fella and I couldn't have wished for a better husband for my baby daughter, but I've told him he's only got shares in her. I said in my speech that my mum would have been proud that her little man was giving away his little daughter to such a great bloke. Not only is he a grand lad, but he gave me the best wedding present I could have wished for: a pair of grandfather slippers, with the comfy fluff inside!

In his groom's speech, he told the guests that when I'm

doing my "business", I like to do it in slippers. And then he presented me with a pair of beauties – what more could a man ask for?

Both Becky and Carla have met two great lads and they're both workers as well, which pleases me greatly.

Oh, did I mention who are Carla is engaged to? It's my mate Ryan 'The Undertaker' Vincent. He got down on one knee in the pub one night after a few drinks. I was a tad surprised and said to him: "Look, you silly bastard, you're supposed to get down on one knee to her, not me!"

So now that my second daughter has settled down, my first film role is in the bag and I have my new pair of grandfather slippers, I'm a happy man. I thank my daughters for my happiness after all the shit I've been through. Just recently, they organised a surprise retirement party for me. They invited all the people I hold dear; those who had been there for me through thick and thin. Becky told me to meet her at the Alpha Club, below my gym, for a few drinks, so me and Angie – who was also in on the secret – turned up for what I thought would be a regular Sunday-afternoon natter with the brood.

When I walked into the bar my eyes nearly popped out: dozens of friends and family rose as one to applaud me. At the back of the room was a display of old photographs and newspaper cuttings which mapped out my boxing career from my very first bouts as a cub fighter to the bare-knuckle scraps in my 40s. Becky and Carla had put it all together themselves, bless 'em. I was choked, but I didn't burst out until the really big surprise walked through the door: my old trainer James Walker and former manager Trevor Callaghan, who had travelled from the other end of the country to be at my retirement bash. I gave James and Trevor a big hug and then the tears came gushing out.

Of course, this wasn't the first 'retirement' do I'd had: there have been two or three others down the years, but I've always made a comeback. Will this one be my last? It's hard to say. I know there's still a few bare-knuckle guys out there who want to take me on and whether I'll be able to resist the challenge remains to be seen.

It's hard to retire when you've been in the game for so long, and the buzz I still get when my mates are cheering me on is like a drug. Also, there are a few scores I might want to settle before I finally put my slippers on for good. There's one boy in particular who needs teaching a lesson. His name is Josh Mundy, the guy who knocked Matt Thorn out in 20 seconds at B-Bad 3, the one I missed. He was being such a braggart in the ring and when he knocked Matt out he was dancing around him, shouting: "Get up! Get up!"

If I ever get inside the ring with Mr Mundy he'll do very well to get up once I've clobbered him with a few Josephs. Treating a nice kid like Matt with such disrespect is way out of line.

In the meantime, I will continue to get my nose bashed in by The Clobberer and my shins kicked black and blue by The Nasty One. I will go down the cellar and trade elbows with The Bull.

I will continue to have periods of depression; I will continue to protect my family from all the horrors of this world. I will continue to love my children and grandchildren with all my soul.

I will continue to work like a dog for the good of my family; grieve my mother and mourn my nephew. I will continue to continue.

Editor's Notes: Radford the Anachronism

When Dave Radford talks about boxing and his career, he is unequivocal about what has made him one of the most feared bare-knucklers of his era.

It's not the fearsome left hook he calls 'Joseph', nor the big right he calls 'Herbert': it's a big heart.

One can talk until the cows come home about training, technique, fitness, guile and speed, but, according to Radford, if the ticker's not big enough, you might as well call it a day.

Radford's professional record is by no means outstanding – poor early management and a terrible accident made sure of that. Nor is his record on the bare-knuckle or cage scene ever going to trouble the record books.

So what makes the former shaft-sinker from a small town in West Yorkshire such an alluring figure and irresistible muse? The answer lies in his unique, infectious and somewhat contradictory personality. This is a man who goes the distance with world champions but gets involves in pub brawls; a born scrapper who thinks nothing of damaging opponents with a mighty left hook but can't watch youngsters fighting without being reduced to tears.

An enigma to his very core, Radford has the complexity of the classic prize-fighters of yore: a warm family man and cold fighting machine; a gentle soul and pugnacious warrior; an old-fashioned gent who doesn't swear in front of women but might turn up at the odd cock fight.

A proud Yorkshireman with an Irish fighting heart, he shares blood lines with some of the gipsy fighters he takes to the cleaners on the straw. His own brand of straight, stand-up boxing harks back to the days of the old gentlemen fighters of the Georgian and Victorian eras. He's the bare-knuckle prototype: a fearless lion heart; a fighter so primitive in his style, as with his approach to life, that he's something of a throwback.

There's something of the Jem Mace about Radford the indefatigable warrior. Mace, one of the old Victorian fighters so beloved of the Hemsworth man, was twice English middleweight bare-knuckle champion between 1861 and 1866. Radford, who may well end up fighting into his late 40s, will take inspiration from the fact that the Norfolk man - who was known as 'The Gypsy' despite fervently denying any Romany roots - fought for 35 years until well into his 70s, and took part in an exhibition bout at the age of 79!

The Beast wants the bare-knuckle scene to recapture the magic of Mace and the pugnacity of the early fist merchants of Ancient Rome and Greece. The sport can be traced right back to the ancient Minoans, a Bronze Age civilisation who held boxing contests as far back as 4,000 BC on the island now known as Crete.

In 776 BC, the Greeks, who absolutely loved the sport, included boxing in the first-ever Olympic games. As a precursor to the wraps worn by modern-day knucklers, the Greek fighters wore ox-hide thongs which they wrapped around their hands to protect their knuckles.

Two millennia ago, death was a common occurrence in the boxing arena, whose stellar cast included Greek warlords who fought for mules and Roman pugilists who battered one another senseless for the prize of a bull.

Today the sport is reviled by many as an underground den of iniquity, a sordid arena for barbarians and bar-room brawlers. It is a world synonymous with barbarity and criminality, and inextricably linked to the gipsy fighters bashing each other's heads in on deserted lanes for family pride as well as hard cash. And yet there is so much more to the scene and its protagonists than meets the eye. Some boxing purists argue that it is, in fact, the truest form of pugilism and one that may end up rescuing boxing from its current malaise and the money-grubbing moguls of the gloved discipline. Radford and his ilk are living proof that the fist game is not the sole preserve of gipsy grudge matches and family vendettas.

Perhaps a fair proportion of the sport's detractors are blithely unaware of its fine traditions. Over the past 2,000 years, bare-knuckle boxing has been graced by fighters from all backgrounds, from the English nobility to Georgian market traders and the prize fighters of imperial Rome.

In England, the fight game had accrued so much kudos by the halcyon years of the 1720s that it was literally a sport for kings. Yet the man chiefly responsible for the sport's meteoric rise from back-street brawling to popular acclaim was an illiterate butcher from Oxfordshire called James Figg, the first recognised English champion.

Figg's sublime skills as a boxer and fencer made him the toast of Georgian society. He went to seek his fortune in London after the Earl of Peterborough spotted him giving an exhibition in the arts of boxing and fencing on his village green in Thame, Oxfordshire. So impressed was the earl by Figg's prodigious talents that he summoned him to London immediately, so confident was he that he had unearthed a rough diamond.

Back then, in the early 1800s, London was a hissing, spitting cesspit where casual violence was rife and criminality the norm. Figg entered this nest of vipers as an anonymous butcher, but soon became a household name as he took on all-comers and carved them up like so many cuts of lamb. In 1719, he opened a huge boxing academy in Adam and Eve Court where he taught anyone who coughed up enough cash for the privilege.

Figg never lost a fight and was the undisputed champion of England until his retirement in 1730. Due to his unprecedented achievements in the knuckle game, his pivotal role in bringing the sport out of the back alleys and tawdry taverns of London is without question.

When he died, at the age of about 40, in December 1734, his fame was such that his passing warranted a full-page obituary in Gentleman's Magazine, the Georgian society bible.

After Figg, there was a clutch of fighters with serious claims to the English knuckle throne. Tom Pipes and George Gretting were contenders, as were Jack Broughton and Tom Smallwood. Also prominent among the early English fighters was John Smith, known as Buckhorse, who was renowned as much for his ugliness as his pugilistic prowess.

Buckhorse became something of a celebrity in Georgian society despite - or perhaps because of - his hideous features, most notably a big, bulbous head. The unsightly Londoner - a petty thief who was brought up in the notorious Lewkner's Lane area - displayed a rare aptitude for pugilism through his appearances at Figg's Academy, under the auspices of Broughton. Against all odds, Buckhorse enjoyed a blessed existence and, surprisingly, was a hit with the ladies too. He met his end, somewhat ignominiously, in a ditch, clutching a bottle of gin.

By the mid-19th century, the naysayers who had held the sport in check for so many years were becoming less vociferous, their dissenting voices gradually drowned out by the general buzz emanating from the noble art's cheerleaders. The introduction of the Queensbury Rules in 1865 ushered in the now-commonplace three-minute rounds with a minute's interval. Gloves were obligatory, as were padded ringside stanchions and 10-second counts after a knockdown.

With gloved boxing now in the ascendancy, the bare-knuckle scene disappeared from the public eye and went underground. But there was one man who straddled both the bare-fist and glove disciplines like a colossus in the late 19th and early 20th centuries. His name was Bob Fitzsimmons - Radford's mate. In his prime, Fitzsimmons was the undisputed king of both formats. Known as The Freckled Wonder, he was one of the cleverest and deadliest hitters of his or any other era. Arriving on the scene during the transitional period from bare fist to gloves, the copper-haired Cornishman, who had Irish blood and lived for a time as an ex-pat in New Zealand, was equally adept at both disciplines, but it was with the gloves that he achieved lasting fame. A gangly six-footer, he held world-title belts in three different divisions at various points in a long and distinguished career spanning 34 years.

Though a middleweight by trade, Fitzsimmons could mix it with the heavies too, and won a disputed version of the world-heavyweight title when he defeated Irish-American Peter Maher in 1896.

Many among the boxing cognoscenti regarded the Cornishman as the greatest pound-for-pound boxer who ever lived, as well as the best-ever body puncher among the heavyweights.

Nat Fleischer, founder of The Ring magazine, said 'Fitz' had the best left hook he had ever seen.

'Gentleman Jim' Corbett, whom Fitzsimmons defeated in New York in defence of his world-heavyweight title, paid perhaps the greatest tribute to his old foe: "For his weight and inches, he was the greatest fighter that ever drew on a glove."

And Gene Tunney, the Irish-American former world-heavyweight champion who retired undefeated in 1928, said that "Fitz could unleash terrific blows for his size, and it is conceivable that he could have taken (Joe) Louis…".

So there we have it: Radford's man was arguably The Greatest - though Ali, Sugar Ray and Joe Louis might have had something to say about that! One thing we can say with near certainty is that Fitzsimmons was the last of the great gentleman fighters who proved themselves with the fists as well as the gloves. The Freckled Wonder, The Belligerent Butcher and the mighty John L. Sullivan have long since gone, their remarkable feats shrouded in the mists of time. But what is their legacy?

Up until recently, the bare-knuckle scene has been confined to rickety old barns, dank cellars, dung-covered cow fields and shady bars, attracting dozens, not thousands, of spectators, and viewed with great suspicion by the great majority, as an arena for barbarians; so far removed from the halcyon days of the Figg era that it is almost unrecognisable as the same sport.

So what now for the much-maligned knuckle art? Is it destined to remain underground and illicit as it has effectively been since the days when the 'Merrie Monarch' King Charles II left the throne? Will it remain largely the preserve of the big gipsy families whose men fight grudge matches against enemy clans on behalf of their elders? Or will it, perhaps, come out into the open once again?

Certainly there are enough people in the right circles trying to make that happen and many willing fighters out there – Radford included - ready to take up the cudgels to make it a popular pastime once again.

Andy Topliffe and his partner Clare Monaghan are two of the chief agitators in the UK doing their best to bring the bare-fist game out of its underground habitat and back into packed-out arenas. Topliffe, an ex-knuckler who runs B-Bad Promotions, is currently working on something called Field Rage, where the participants fight in a lane or grassed area with an ambulance and a doctor in tow should any of the fighters get seriously hurt. The objective is to legitimise the bare-knuckle game and make it safer.

Topliffe recently spoke to a national tabloid newspaper about his campaign to bring the sport out into the open and expressed his dismay that the knuckle scene was still a pariah in the sporting world, whereas cage-fighting and MMA - where fighters can use elbows, knees and kicks – are legitimate disciplines deemed suitable for general viewing.

"Bare-knuckle boxing has been around for 1,500 years in the UK and was our first martial art," Topliffe told the Sunday Sport.

"People view bare-knuckle fighting as something bad, but all the fighters can use is their hands. The men who come to this sport want to fight toe-to-toe, man to man.

"It's crazy that in MMA you can kick your opponent in the face, knee them, choke them or stamp on their head, yet this is legal and bare-knuckle fighting isn't.

"You can do a lot more damage with a foot, a knee or an elbow than you can with a fist, and we want to get this ancient sport back into the mainstream, where it belongs."

Topliffe has been lobbying local councils asking for permission to stage BKB events in public venues that have already hosted MMA bouts. He's also trying to form a BKB governing body and been given a licence to open a gym in Loughborough where budding bare-knucklers can learn the ropes. The idea is to generate a broader pool of talent which BKB has been lacking these past 100 years.

At the third B-Bad show, in February 2012, the organisers were able to use a proper canvassed ring for the first time. Intriguingly, Topliffe says he has also been in secret talks with two unnamed American fighters who are mulling over the possibility of hopping over the pond to fight at the next bare-knuckle event. Understandably, then, the boxing promoter waxes optimistic about BKB's future.

"We are moving forward and times are good for UK BKB," he said on B-Bad's Facebook page.

"We haven't been able to get weight divisions yet but we are hoping to have our own league up and running soon, with all fighters having a rank position and a belt to fight for. We are getting there slowly."

He added: "I have researched BKB in statute and gone over the Queensbury Rules: there is no statute denying BKB (legality), and although modern rules say gloves must be worn, there is no compulsion under the rule other than in championship bouts."

Radford, once a professional glove boxer, would agree on this point: he dreams of the day when he'll be able to fight in a properly-organised bare-knuckle event in one of his local pubs. In truth, he's convinced he's missed his ship again, because, even if it does happen, we're not likely to see truly-legal bare-knuckle boxing in public venues in the UK for another 10 years at least. Perhaps the BKB movement is secretly resigned to this and certainly there have been rumours of late that they may be changing tack and trying to legitimise the sport by taking a leaf out of the MMA book – namely by introducing kicking, choking, elbowing and head-butting. The rumours have not been confirmed, but Radford doesn't like the idea one bit.

"I'm all for them bringing the bare-knuckle game back into the open and I would love one day to be able to fight in front of my friends in a legitimate, open setting," he says.

"But the whole idea, initially, was for pure, bare-fist fighting like in the old days. Anything other than that would defeat the purpose."

Cage Amateurs UK, a group set up to support MMA fighters, has also espoused BKB and is doing its best to get bare-knuckle the same kind of recognition that mixed martial arts have enjoyed for a good number of years. Cage Amateurs' Daniel Towers and Jon Pepperel made a film of the B-Bad 2 event at Hinckley in what was their first experience of a bare-knuckle show. They were expecting a dust-up in a cow field or a ramshackle old barn, but were astonished to find themselves in a spotless bar with no barking dogs or cow dung in sight.

Towers wrote enthusiastically about his maiden bare-knuckle venture on the Cage Amateurs website.

"We headed off for what we thought would be a cold, wet afternoon in some barn in the middle of a field somewhere," he said.

"We had images of those 'windmill fests' you see on Youtube where each fight lasts half an hour or so, but the fighters end up with next-to-no injuries despite the large number of blows being exchanged between them.

"Nothing could have been further from the truth! In reality, we found ourselves at a well-organised show complete with hot running water and electricity, and certainly there was no barn in sight. I confessed to promoter Andy Topliffe what we had initially expected and was met with a fair bit of merriment!"

Yet despite the optimism of Topliffe et al, it remains undeniable that, for whatever reason, the knuckle scene in the UK is still struggling to make itself heard, even at a time when the gloved sport is at an all-time low due to dodgy promoters, sub-standard fighters and the inexorable rise of mixed martial arts. But, in the States, BKB is knocking at the door louder than ever – and the general public seems to be listening. There is a firm belief among the bare-knuckle promoters Stateside that the public, tired of the hyperbole and insipidness that has dogged the gloved game for a generation, is crying out for a return to the old days of toe-to-toe, no-nonsense bare-knuckle fighting.

While the stigma attached to the knuckle game in Britain still clings to the sport like a limpet, the World Bare Knuckle Boxing Association (WBKBA) is making great strides in legitimising the fist game over in the States. The organisation was formed by a small group of aficionados led by world bare-knuckle champion Bobby Gunn. Group president Chris Cella said recently that he believed the sport could become as big, if not bigger, than gloved boxing and MMA.

The optimistic noises coming from America are starting to echo in the UK, albeit not as loudly. One former British knuckler recently told a regional daily newspaper that he felt the sport was on the cusp of being accepted into the mainstream. Michael Blackett, from Teesdale in the North East, is part of the campaign to legitimise the sport in the UK and is convinced it will return to popular acclaim.

"We're determined to bust the myth that it's brutal," he told the Northern Echo newspaper.

"Our long-term goal is to see the end of underground fighting and for this great sport to be completely regulated, making it safer for the fighters and for all concerned.

"There are fights in every city every weekend - not just travellers, but the settled community too. Unfortunately, YouTube only shows fights between Irish travellers. We want to make it above board, sort out the legals – it's the way forward."

If Blackett is to be believed, then the bare-knuckle format might just be in our pubs, clubs and leisure arenas before we know it. That would please Radford no end, but he's in his 44th year now and time may be running out. The broken cheekbones and battered eyes are bad enough, but his memory is an even bigger concern.

As The Beast himself says: "I've taken some proper hammer down the years and it's taken its toll."

Now well into mid-life, can Radford really keep mixing it with the young knuckle terrors of today? Or is he on the road to perdition once again?

Opportunity has already knocked for the Hemsworth man in the States, but he remains a man of his territory. In 2012, he was offered the chance to fight in the US as part of a UK 'dream team' made up of 10 bare-knucklers led by the mighty Quinn McDonagh, but he turned it down on the grounds that he was only interested in consolidating his reputation in his own country.

Back on his own shores, the pugnacious pipe-fitter continues to carry the honour and spirit of the old gentlemen boxers into his every fight, but how much longer can he carry on before the ravages of time make him a danger unto himself?

If fractured bones and ravaged eyes aren't enough to force a well-earned retirement, what's to say he can't go on for another five years? He has the bravery of Buckhorse and Ali's heart to go on fighting well into his 40s, but the former died prematurely and the latter has spent the past 30 years stricken by Parkinson's disease.

Radford's quandary is this: he's addicted to a sport he half-loves and half-loathes. So the question is perhaps not when he will retire, but how.

Before he makes his mind up, he would do well to heed the words of the late boxing scribe Mark Kram, who, in his brilliant work 'Ghosts of Manila: The Fateful Blood Feud Between Muhammad Ali and Joe Frazier', provided a stark reminder (if any were needed) of the dangers inherent in stretching out boxing careers that have already gone on way too long.

Ruminating on how Ali and Frazier's deadly feud effectively reduced both men to ghostly versions of their former selves, Kram wrote: 'No other sport expresses its cost as starkly as boxing does. Each face and brain is a map of risky travel, revealing the length of the trip and all the bad roads.'

The wise words of sagacious sports columnist Hugh McIlvaney might also offer some indication as to what is likely to befall the ageing sportsman whose pride clouds his better judgement and impels him to carry on when clearly the better option is to retire and look back on fond memories.

During the India-versus-England cricket Test series in the winter of 2012, the award-winning scribe pondered whether the great Indian batsman Sachin Tendulkar should finally call it a day at the ripe old age of 39 after a poor run of form which threatened to cast a shadow over a scintillating career with the bat which had yielded over 15,000 Test runs and 51 centuries.

McIlvaney, known as 'The Voice of Sport', said it was time 'The Little Master' quit to spare him the ignominy of finishing perhaps the greatest-ever first-class cricketing career on a bum note.

'He will want to depart before he starts selling his immense talent short,' wrote the award-winning Sunday Times columnist.

'Retirements in cricket are usually more rationally managed than they are in some other sports. Boxing is particularly notorious for destructively wrong-headed reluctance to quit, and all kinds of delusions contribute to bad decisions.

'One of the most offensive fallacies is that the last asset an effective boxer loses is his punch. Since timing is generally crucial to punching power, and timing is eroded by age and wear and tear, that declaration is untenable.

'Mike Tyson, who once hit hard enough to bring down a small building, eventually couldn't hurt a Danny Williams or a Kevin McBride. By then, Tendulkar might have given Tyson trouble.'

My Mate 'The Beast'   A Tribute by George Probert

What can I say that hasn't already been said about my mate 'The Beast'? Well let me try.

I first met him 20 years ago and we've been good friends ever since. He was already an up-and-coming professional boxer when we started working together and I started going with him to training sessions and fights.

It was hard for Dave back then. He had a wife, two small children and a home to pay for. He had to train at least three or four times a week while holding down a full-time job.

He worked hard and trained hard, and would fight anyone put in front of him, sometimes boxers a lot more experienced or even two-to-three stones heavier than him. He never refused a fight and gave everything and more in the ring: sometimes winning, sometimes losing.

Every time he fought with the heart of a warrior. I saw Dave get out-boxed and put down twice in a fight with the "next British champion" Dave Johnson in his home town, but he came back with a shot to win the fight which unfortunately put the kid out of boxing. It just shows the size of Dave's fighting heart.

Outside the ring, Dave has another side to his heart. He is kind and caring towards his family and friends, and has made many friends during his working and fighting career. The man is so easy to get on with and will do anything for anyone.

Dave has had highs and lows in his fighting and working career. He was fortunate to be asked to go to Africa to fight the great Roberto Duran. Dave took the fight with a few hours' notice and went the distance with Duran. Not long after that he returned to work and he and his workmate John Delaney had a very serious accident which resulted in John being paralysed and left Dave with major injuries including six crushed vertebrae. If Dave and John weren't so fit and strong at the time, the pair of them might not be here now.

After a long time recovering, Dave wanted to return to the fight game, but, without a boxing licence, he ventured into

The Cage, where his first opponent was Mike 'The Count' Bisping. Dave took that fight with very little notice and gave a very good account of himself.

After a few more fights in The Cage, he went on to bare-knuckling, in which he still fights at the ripe old age of 44. I've been to 90 per cent of his fights and feel the nerves every time, but Dave has no nerves at all. Before he goes into battle, he's the one cracking jokes and trying to calm *me* down.

Dave has a true fighting heart and is a true gentleman – everyone who has met him would agree. He is my best friend and my hero.

Editor's Acknowledgements

Thank you to my family for all the support and love you have given me down the years.

And to all those who helped me complete this project when I was at my wit's end, in particular all those people without whose technical nous and computer wizadry this book would never have got off the ground.

A special thanks to Rob White of R.L White Photography, whose fantastic action shots show 'The Beast' in full roar; and to Jason Ferdinando, the design genius who made it all possible.

Thanks also to Darren Wiseman of Salesarm and E-shop Creator, whose cajoling kept me going through the lean times; and to Cage Amateurs UK for their support during the making of this autobiography. Thanks also to Owen Ralph of Parkworld.

Most of all, thanks to 'The Beast' himself, whose extraordinary candour and bravery have invested this book with that most crucial ingredient: heart.

Printed in Great Britain
by Amazon.co.uk, Ltd.,
Marston Gate.